WORLD LANGUAGES

JANIS JENSEN
PAUL SANDROCK

A Chapter of the

CURRICULUM
HANDBOOK

REVISED 2005

ASSOCIATION FOR SUPERVISION AND CURRICULUM DEVELOPMENT
ALEXANDRIA, VIRGINIA USA

Association for Supervision and Curriculum Development
1703 N. Beauregard St. • Alexandria, VA 223111714 USA
Telephone: 1-800-933-2723 or 1-703-578-9600 • Fax: 1-703-575-5400
Web site: www.ascd.org • E-mail: member@ascd.org

Gene R. Carter
Executive Director

Kim Pifer
Copyeditor

Michelle Terry
Deputy Executive Director, Program Development

Gary Bloom
Director, Design and Production Services

Nancy Modrak
Director, Publishing

Tracey A. Franklin
Production Manager

John Franklin
Managing Editor, ASCD Curriculum Handbook

Eric Coyle
Production Coordinator

Terrey Hatcher Quindlen
Contributing Editor, ASCD Curriculum Handbook

Keith Demmons
Desktop Publisher

Mary Beth Nielsen
Manager, Editorial Services

Stock #105015

ASCD *Curriculum Handbook* Distribution Policy

WORLD LANGUAGES

LETTER FROM THE EXECUTIVE DIRECTOR

The U.S. Senate has designated 2005 as the Year of Foreign Language Study. Although the recognition is a welcome step in highlighting the importance of language study, the notion of particular dialects as "foreign" continues to be a source of debate. English may once have been the primary language spoken in the United States, but in many parts of the country Spanish is increasingly found alongside it on menus and at ATMs. In places such as Dearborn, Mich., Arabic is extremely prominent, whereas in other parts of our nation, citizens regularly converse in Chinese, French, German, Italian, Japanese, Russian, Vietnamese, and numerous other dialects. With such a wondrous variety, how can we designate as "foreign" that which is simply another part of the patchwork quilt of our multicultural society?

This question is being asked with increasing frequency—not just by educators in schools but by CEOs in boardrooms and conference halls as well. As the global economy continues to expand and take shape, the concept of something as "foreign" is becoming increasingly unclear, because we can no longer divide into two neat categories that which is "ours" and "theirs." Instead, it is evident now as never before that our planet comprises people of many colors and flavorings, each of which will play a critical role in the future of our students.

I had an opportunity to discuss that role earlier this year when I addressed the Kansas Committee for International Education in the Schools about the effects of globalization and the importance of preparing our students to compete in the world economy. In my speech, I examined how the marketplace of ideas and instantaneous dissemination of knowledge is placing greater demands not just on our students but also on our teachers. Preparing our students for tomorrow is a critical task that grows more challenging with each passing year. Middle

school students, for example, may find themselves in another 15 or 20 years heading offices in parts of Asia that 20 or 30 years ago might have been headquartered in America's heartland. Time is a luxury that tomorrow's workers may not have, and decisions that once had to be made by executives in offices will have to be made locally by personnel in the field if companies are to remain competitive. Competitive advantage will belong to those who can communicate effectively and quickly with people from different backgrounds and cultures, and our students must be prepared to lead the way.

Of course, the importance of being able to express oneself clearly has always been at the forefront of every teacher's mind. And nowhere has this focus on the importance of communication been more powerful than in the classrooms of those tasked with teaching our children how to read, speak, and think in the many languages of our world. For years, those in the world language profession have argued passionately about the need to be able to speak in more than one language. With the new global economy, however, people will need to be fluent in several languages, not just two. E-mail, faxes, and videoconferences may enable us to share information more easily; however, if shared methods of talking and communicating are absent, all the technology in the world will not help the exchange of thoughts and ideas. Those who are able to express themselves proficiently will be the true leaders of tomorrow's economy; those who cannot will soon find themselves marginalized by those who can. The world does not wait for people to catch up; it instead rewards those who plan and think with foresight today.

The importance of preparing our children for the international marketplace is something that Janis Jensen and Paul Sandrock have highlighted in this *Curriculum Handbook* chapter on world languages. Using their combined skills and experiences, they have rewritten this chapter for the 21st century and outlined a number of the latest trends and challenges confronting world language instructors. The result is a remarkable work that we know will be an excellent tool for your teachers and educators.

Although we in the education profession may cheer the designation of 2005 as the Year of Foreign Language Study in the United States, we know that the importance of language study does not coincide with dates on a calendar. The world our students will one day inherit will be one of astounding promise and potential, but they will be able to take advantage of its offerings only if we infuse them with the knowledge that enables them to appreciate and use the wonders that this world will offer them. Preparing them will require vision, initiative, and strong leadership—and it will require the careful and guiding hand of those tasked with helping prepare them for this journey: their teachers.

Gene R. Carter
Executive Director, ASCD

I. OVERVIEW

Thanks to a number of technological advances—ease of travel over vast distances, instantaneous telephone connections, and the Internet—interacting with individuals from other countries has become commonplace for a great number of people. This unprecedented accessibility to other languages and cultures—whether for social, political, business, governmental, or humanitarian purposes—has created what is now universally referred to as the "global community" and is calling into question our concept of what is "foreign." Our economy has brought workers from abroad to America and, conversely, sent jobs to countries around the world. Our health is affected by conditions and events in China, Africa, South America, and Britain. Sales representatives, bank employees, and computer technicians who provide us with everyday home and business services may be citizens of other countries living abroad. Furthermore, changing demographics worldwide have resulted in increasing interaction with individuals from other cultures who speak a variety of languages on a day-to-day basis, in the home community as well as in the workplace.

TIME TO REPOSITION WORLD LANGUAGES

In this context, the term "foreign language" is a misnomer and the use of the term "foreign" to describe the field of second-language education no longer seems to adequately reflect the interconnectedness of the world's peoples, their languages, and their cultures. "Foreign" also denotes exclusion, isolation, and alienation, rather than a sense of acceptance, collaboration, and community. The term is especially ill-fitting in the United States, which has been characterized by constant and ever-increasing multilingualism throughout its history (Herman, 2002). The 2000 U.S. census, for example, showed that 10 percent of the population—24.8 million

people—is foreign-born, the largest number in American history. As of July 2003, the population of Hispanics had reached 39.9 million, accounting for about one-half of the 9.4 million residents added to the nation's population since the 2000 census. Further, new estimates released by the U.S. Census Bureau in June 2004 predict the nation's Hispanic and Asian populations will continue to grow at much faster rates than the population as a whole (Mok, 2004). Hence, the languages and cultures of the world beyond the United States' borders can no longer be considered "foreign." This realization has caused educators in many states to shift their thinking and, as a result, to adopt the term "world languages," renaming the discipline to reflect a world where peoples and cultures are in a constant state of movement and interaction, and where knowledge of a world language or languages will enable students to think and communicate globally in their future lives as citizens and workers.

In recognition of this era of interconnectedness, this chapter of the *Curriculum Handbook* refers to the languages spoken and taught in the worldwide community as "world languages." (Any appearance of the phrase "foreign language" reflects the wording of the source being referenced.) The term is all-encompassing; it appropriately represents the languages and peoples that make up our present multilingual and multicultural global community, but includes the study of classical languages, thereby reflecting the past as well. Accordingly, this world languages curriculum chapter focuses on trends in second-language education in the United States, as well as in other countries, while underscoring the important role language learning plays in students' core curricula across the globe.

The renaming of this area of the curriculum may seem largely symbolic, but it reflects a real paradigm shift in thinking about *who* is studying other languages, *when* language instruction should take place, *what* is being studied in language classrooms, and *how* language instruction is delivered and assessed. It introduces the idea of *inclusivity* to an area of study previously dominated by the idea of *exclusivity*. It also underscores the need to create a different frame of mind among the American public about the value of language learning in order to engage widespread support for the development of long-sequence, well-articulated K–12 second-language programs.

Who is studying other languages?

With the advent of the standards movement and the adoption of national standards for second-language study (National Standards in Foreign Language Education Project, 1996 and 1999), brought about through a collaborative effort of the American Council on the Teaching of Foreign Languages (ACTFL) and other language-specific organizations, the traditional population of students selected to study world languages has changed dramatically. Many states have embraced the national standards document and acknowledge the value of language study for *all* students, whether they are college-bound, career-focused, English language learners, students with special needs, or students from diverse socioeconomic backgrounds. However, in past—and even in current—practice, college-bound students have made up the greatest percentage of the student population studying a second language. Other students, such as those with special needs, have been discouraged from participating in world language programs. Students in the mainstream middle school population, in particular, have frequently been denied participation because their standardized test scores weren't considered high enough or because of average or below-average past academic performance—perceived indicators of an inability to learn a language. This practice directly contradicts the advice given by language acquisition experts, who emphasize several guiding principles in considering language learning for all:

- Language learning is an innate human capability, and, as such, cognitive ability should not be a prerequisite for determining whether a student can effectively acquire a second language;

- If a child functions in one language, he is already a viable candidate to function in other languages; and

- Ability to function in the native language legitimately expands the student's candidacy as a learner of other languages (De Mado, 1995).

The historically exclusionary selection process for world language study is gradually becoming passé in more and more schools as familiarity with research that justifies the inclusion of all students in the language classroom increases among educators in the field (McColl, 2000; McKeown, 2004; National Council of State Supervisors for Languages, 2002; Wilson, 2004; Wing, 1996). In addition, educators are coming to realize that the benefits attained by these students through such study extend beyond the practical one of proficiency in a nonnative language to cognitive, academic, and effective benefits—particularly attitudinal benefits, such as fostering respect and appreciation of cultural diversity. The view of *who* learns another language has therefore shifted from offering language study as an academic pursuit for an elite student population to offering language study as a life skill to be acquired by all students, regardless of their post-high school plans. It incorporates a new world of language learners.

When should language instruction take place?

When students begin the study of a language is an important factor in ensuring success for all learners. Recently released state and national studies continue to recommend longer, uninterrupted sequences of language study beginning at the earliest grades to achieve higher levels of linguistic and cultural proficiency (American Council on Education, 2002; National Association of State Boards of Education [NASBE], 2003; North Carolina Department of Public Instruction, 2003; U.S. Department of Defense, 2004). To date, however, considerable debate exists over whether children are better language learners than adults. Although research in the field of neuropsychology suggests that the neural plasticity of the younger brain does make it uniquely suited to the task of language acquisition (Huttenlocher, 1994), adult learners obviously can and do become competent and fluent speakers of other languages. Hoff-Ginsberg (1998) maintains that the key question for educators is how to take advantage of what appears to be children's special capacity for language acquisition. Engaging that capacity clearly must lie within the goals and design of the elementary world language curriculum.

When students begin learning second languages early in quality programs, they have the time to internalize the sounds of a language, accumulate a bank of vocabulary and phrases, and develop language-learning strategies that will lead to greater language proficiency when they continue language study at the secondary level. This is especially important given what research tells us about the need for the brain to connect new learning with learning already stored in memory (Caine & Caine, 1997). Much like learning in other areas of the curriculum, students benefit from starting early and continuing through a long sequence of learning that grows and deepens as they mature (Haas, 1998). Myriam Met (2000), past president of the National Network for Early Language Learning, also emphasizes the need for long sequences of study as an integral part of early schooling, when the integration of content and language learning occurs easily, along with the development of positive attitudes toward people who speak other languages and represent other cultures. The issue of *when* language instruction should take place has therefore evolved from a narrow, prescriptive time frame of two years of instruction at the secondary level to a broader and more flexible time frame that may occur at multiple entry points at the elementary level.

What is being studied in the world language classroom?

The implementation of standards has also redefined the content of world language instruction. The focal point of standards-driven instruction is meaningful communication and the facilitation of genuine interaction among students through classroom activities that are embedded in authentic, real-life contexts. Most of you reading this handbook chapter probably remember that when you began the study of another language, you assumed you would acquire skills that would enable you to communicate with other speakers of that language. After all, communication was the stated goal of language instruction, both in course descriptions and curricula. What you probably experienced, however, was an emphasis on language lexicon, syntax, morphology, and phonology. And, not surprisingly, your learning outcomes reflected the goals of instruction, not those of the curriculum: you knew how to conjugate verbs, analyze abstract grammatical structures, and translate sentences and paragraphs with grammatical accuracy using long lists of memorized vocabulary, but very few of you could communicate at even a basic survival level in the "real" world.

What should today's students expect to be able to do when they study another language? In standards-driven world language classrooms, students should expect to engage in relevant, age-appropriate communicative tasks that emerge from nonacademic areas of interest and importance as well as from academic content in other curricular areas. The standards guiding the teaching of languages (see Figure 1) are summarized as the five Cs (National Standards in Foreign Language Education Project, 1996):

- Communication (exchanging, understanding, and presenting information and ideas)

- Cultures (understanding the products, practices, and perspectives of people who speak the language)

- Connections (acquiring information from other cultures and learning content from other disciplines)

- Comparisons (comparing other languages and cultures to one's own)

- Communities (using language beyond the classroom for lifelong enjoyment and enrichment)

This represents a dramatic change in content for the world language classroom. Rather than being the primary focus of study, the second language instead becomes a means through which areas of student interest are explored. Content in the grade-level curriculum is learned, reinforced, or enhanced *while* second-language skills are acquired and developed. For example, 8th grade students in a middle school Spanish class learn Spanish by studying a thematic unit on global warming, concentrating their study on its potential economic and cultural effects in Spanish-speaking countries. The traditional view of Spanish as a "subject" area has changed in this case, because Spanish grammar and structure are not the focus of instruction. This is not

---

Figure 1
Standards for Foreign Language Learning

Communication: Communicate in Languages Other Than English
Standard 1.1: Students engage in conversations, provide and obtain information, express feelings and emotions, and exchange opinions.
Standard 1.2: Students understand and interpret written and spoken language on a variety of topics.
Standard 1.3: Students present information, concepts, and ideas to an audience of listeners or readers on a variety of topics.

Cultures: Gain Knowledge and Understanding of Other Cultures
Standard 2.1: Students demonstrate an understanding of the relationship between the practices and perspectives of the culture studied.
Standard 2.2: Students demonstrate an understanding of the relationship between the products and perspectives of the culture studied.

Connections: Connect with Other Disciplines and Acquire Information
Standard 3.1: Students reinforce and further their knowledge of other disciplines through the foreign language.
Standard 3.2: Students acquire information and recognize the distinctive viewpoints that are available only through study of the foreign language and its cultures.

Comparisons: Develop Insight into the Nature of Language and Culture
Standard 4.1: Students demonstrate understanding of the nature of language through comparisons of the language studied and their own.
Standard 4.2: Students demonstrate understanding of the concept of culture through comparisons of the cultures studied and their own.

Communities: Participate in Multilingual Communities at Home and Around the World
Standard 5.1: Students use the language both within and beyond the school setting.
Standard 5.2: Students show evidence of becoming lifelong learners by using the language for personal enjoyment and enrichment.

Source: From *Standards for Foreign Language Learning: Preparing for the 21st Century* (p. 9), by the American Council on the Teaching of Foreign Languages (ACTFL), 1996, Yonkers, NY: ACTFL. Copyright 1996 by the ACTFL. Reprinted with permission.

to say that structure is ignored, but student acquisition of language structures emerges naturally from the communicative tasks and assessments designed around the theme of the unit—in this case, global warming. Shifting the focus from linguistic content to real-world content allows students to use language to obtain information and knowledge for social purposes, which is critical to acquiring language. This approach also motivates students to communicate and enables them to better retain concepts, transfer concepts across disciplines, and apply them to real-life situations.

Using content from other subject areas in the teaching of languages is not a new concept. Dual immersion, immersion, bilingual, and English as a second language (ESL) models of instruction have used this approach for decades, and its success is documented by research. With the introduction of the standards for language learning, however, this concept is beginning to extend to language teaching in other settings, especially in elementary and middle school world language programs. In these programs, a content-enriched (the language teacher uses concepts from the general curriculum to enrich language instruction) or a content-based (the language teacher assumes responsibility for teaching certain areas of the grade-level curriculum) approach is often used.

In content-enriched or content-related programs, language instruction includes concepts from other subject areas, such as science, math, or social studies—as seen in the global warming example. Much like the student population, the content of the world language classroom has become inclusive. The focus of the language curriculum has expanded, moving from a narrow approach that says the content of language instruction is *only* language, to encompass the idea that language is an effective tool to communicate content. World languages can no longer be viewed as an isolated area of the curriculum in which the learning is set apart from learning that is taking place in other content areas. Learning through languages other than English has now become part of all student learning, heightening the importance and visibility of world languages within the entire school community.

How is language instruction delivered and assessed?

Students come to world language classrooms with different interests and varying intelligences and learning styles. Instructional activities and assessments should reflect these needs. Teaching and learning strategies used in the world language classroom are multifaceted and based on students' active involvement with their own learning. Classrooms once limited to a single text as the primary instructional resource and pencil-and-paper assessments have transitioned into classrooms that use the latest technologies to provide culturally authentic materials as the foundation for the creation of meaningful communicative tasks. Students work collaboratively on multistage projects that have a real-world purpose, similar to those they will encounter in the community or the workplace.

World language assessments reflect a similar focus and mirror performance-based instructional activities taking place in the classroom on a daily basis. They allow students to demonstrate what they know and can do, showing the evolution of their growing language proficiency in multiple ways using real-world tasks. Although discrete-point quizzes and tests are efficient and objective, they do not assess the application of knowledge and skills in real-world situations—the ability to communicate orally in an appropriate cultural context or the ability to create with language. The culture of testing world languages has, therefore, shifted from reliance on assessing only what students *know* through objective tests to assessing what students can *do* through multiple measures and perspectives. "Because of the broad range of behaviors and functions associated with [second] language proficiency, performance assessment would have to entail a variety of assessment methods in a variety of content [areas]" (Donato, 1998). The new testing culture is now inextricably connected to a wide range of content and a variety of instructional strategies practiced in K–12 classrooms and, most importantly, has the primary goal of emphasizing achievement in *all* learners.

WORLD LANGUAGES ARE AN ESSENTIAL PART OF A BALANCED CURRICULUM

The critical need to include the study of world languages in the core curriculum has been consistently reiterated in recent reports, studies, journals, and articles published by the media within the past several years. In addition, the study of world languages has been included in the list of core subjects prescribed by the No Child Left Behind Act (NCLB; U.S. Department of Education, 2001). Using the law's provisions for the proliferation and improvement of world languages as a core area of study, however, is not common practice. The NASBE, in response to the concerns of its members about the status of both arts and world languages study in the United States, examined the current trend in American education policy of narrowing the curriculum to focus on federal and state accountability mandates. Interestingly, this trend does not reflect support from parents and the public at large for a comprehensive education that includes the study of academic areas in addition to English language arts and mathematics (Hayward & Siaya, 2001).

The 2003 NASBE report, titled *The Complete Curriculum: Ensuring a Place for the Arts and Foreign Languages in America's Schools*, provides a compilation of research on the cognitive and affective benefits of the study of other languages and the advantages of early language learning; presents an overview of the current state of world language education in U.S. schools; and makes recommendations

to its members for the creation of policies that facilitate the inclusion of world language instruction in states' core curricula. Among these recommendations are the following:

1. Adopt high-quality licensure requirements for staff in the arts and foreign languages that are aligned with student standards in these subject areas.
2. Ensure adequate time for high-quality professional staff development in the arts and foreign languages.
3. Ensure adequate staff expertise at the state agency in the areas of arts and foreign languages.
4. Incorporate both the arts and foreign languages into core graduation requirements, while simultaneously increasing the number of credits for graduation.
5. Encourage higher-education institutions to increase standards for admission and include arts and foreign language courses when calculating high school grade point averages.
6. Incorporate arts and foreign language learning into K–12 standards, curriculum frameworks, and course requirements. Also, encourage local school districts to incorporate the arts and foreign languages into instruction in the early years, whenever possible.
7. Advocate continued development of curriculum materials for the arts and foreign languages from the textbook publishing industry.
8. Incorporate all core-subject areas, including the arts and foreign languages, into the improvement strategies promoted by No Child Left Behind.
9. Urge the National Assessment Governing Board to increase the frequency of administration of the National Assessment of Educational Progress (NAEP) assessments for both the arts and foreign languages.

10. Urge the U.S. Congress and state legislatures to make a greater commitment to the arts and foreign languages (pp. 5–25).

In *Academic Atrophy: The Condition of the Liberal Arts in America's Public Schools,* Claus von Zastrow (2004), senior program director of the Learning First Alliance, reports on the waning commitment of time and resources for teaching the liberal arts in the United States, especially in schools with high-minority populations. The report is based on the results of a survey of 1,000 principals that explored K–12 students' access to a liberal arts curriculum in schools in Illinois, Maryland, New Mexico, and New York. Approximately three-quarters of the principals surveyed reported increases in instructional time for reading, writing, and mathematics—all subject areas for which their schools are held accountable by NCLB. Similar increases were also found in professional development for these three areas. A decreased commitment was reported for the arts, foreign languages, and elementary social studies. For foreign languages, both increases (11 percent) and decreases (9 percent) were reported in low-minority schools, but in high-minority schools, 23 percent of the principals reported decreases in foreign language instruction (p. 17). Most of these principals reported that instructional time had decreased greatly, and only 9 percent reported increases in foreign language instruction. In high-minority schools, 29 percent of principals expected further decreases in the future, and half of these expected the decreases to be large. In contrast, in low-minority schools, only 14 percent predicted future declines. The report concluded that "the possibility that minorities are more likely to experience a narrowing of the curriculum raises important questions of educational equity" (p. 9). Eliminating such inequity—specifically, narrowing the achievement gap in mathematics and reading among minority students—is one of NCLB's goals,

an aspiration that seems poorly served by disproportionately decreased instruction in foreign languages and the arts in high-minority schools.

Shuler (2003) further builds the case that schools lose their educational balance when they cease to emphasize the needs of the whole child. "Curriculum for the 21st century must cultivate a variety of potentials and possibilities that are of long-term value, which enrich students in ways aesthetic and interpersonal as well as financial" (p. 45). The role of world languages in the core curriculum is difficult to dispute when viewed in this context. As language learners, students take an active role in constructing meaning from their personal experiences, an approach that reflects the philosophy and beliefs of educating the whole child. Moreover, language learning provides students with knowledge and skills across a range of subjects, not just those that are tested.

According to the American Council on Education (2002), "The United States must invest in an educational infrastructure that produces knowledge of languages and cultures, and must be able to steadily train a sufficient and diverse pool of American students to meet the needs of government agencies, the private sector, and education itself" (p. 7). "Developing global competence is a long-term undertaking and must begin at an early age, especially for foreign language acquisition" (p. 10). A curriculum that excludes the study of world languages does not meet the current demands of globalization; it does not prepare our children for the roles they will play as adults and workers in an interdependent world.

Despite the compelling rationale for the inclusion of world languages as an essential component of the core curriculum by policymakers, educators, and the government and business communities, the appropriate resources to ensure such inclusion are not being allocated. Catharine Keatly (2004), associate director of the National Capital Language

Resource Center, reports, "Total funding for foreign language education in the U.S. Department of Education (ED) budget in 2003 was a maximum of $85,425,469, which constitutes 0.15 percent of the overall ED budget. In other words, for each $100 spent by the Department of Education in 2003 . . . 15 cents . . . was spent on foreign language education" (p. 15).

CREATING A NEW FRAME FOR THE VALUE OF LANGUAGE LEARNING

How do Americans react to specific reforms and arguments advanced by education advocates with respect to issues such as language learning? A 2003 study reporting on how Americans view international education, conducted for the American Forum for Global Education and the Asia Society by the FrameWorks Institute (Bales, 2004, pp. 1–19), yielded some interesting findings. Although the goal of the study was to evaluate current thinking about ways to engage the American public in supporting and prioritizing programs and policies to improve students' international skills, the results of the study are applicable on a broader scale to world languages and other areas. In the study, researchers used a unique perspective on communicating social issues—strategic frame analysis—to assess public thinking.

Strategic frame analysis is based on decades of research in the social and cognitive sciences and maintains that people use mental shortcuts that rely on "frames," or small sets of internalized concepts and values, that allow them to give meaning to new information. When education advocates communicate to the public, they have the option of either repeating or breaking these dominant frames of thinking, which can be triggered by different messages or images and have a profound influence on decisions or opinions. When educators effectively communicate about an issue, such as the incorporation of world languages study into the core cur-

riculum, people look beyond the dominant frame of thinking to consider a different perspective.

The study found that the public views international education as a luxury or a set of skills that can be postponed to postsecondary education, especially in a system of education perceived to be failing at the basics. Researchers also found that the public views the reforms necessary to achieve international education as additive, rather than transformative. Clearly, their findings have implications for the study of world languages as well, especially in light of the general perception that learning languages other than English is not an essential component of the core curriculum and certainly not important enough to be included across the K–12 spectrum.

So how can educators reframe this type of thinking? Researchers suggest that rather than make explicit recommendations concerning national security, international relations, the economy, or lack of student knowledge, educators instead present the argument for the study of world languages in a way that reflects a new, more inclusive view of the world, the United States' role in it, and the opportunities such study would provide today's students. They further advise beginning public communications with vivid examples of schools that are making the transformation to international education. They underscore the importance of defining the difference between what currently exists and the vision of what needs to be developed in order to encompass a global perspective, thereby assigning accountability to the system.

Rather than narrowly addressing current problems, frames that work best inspire a positive vision of what we could become or achieve. Understanding and respect are frames that achieve the most public buy-in. For example, people recognize the danger of stereotypes and want their children to respect and value other cultures—an objective that makes sense for broad-based education. Interestingly, these findings are consistent across the entire body of FrameWorks Institute research on public attitudes on international issues both before and after September 11. As with the institute's findings regarding the public's view of international education, this information has obvious implications for the study of world languages and can be of great value in helping educators make their case to the public.

Members of the National Council of State Supervisors for Languages (2002), responsible for implementation of K–12 world languages standards in their respective states, make the case for world languages by reframing the value of language learning for state policymakers in the manner suggested by the FrameWorks Institute research. They have changed the order and logic of the argument to reflect the United States' new role in the world and have created a positive vision of what world language education could be, underscoring the need for understanding and respect of other cultures. They propose several critical steps for educators and policymakers:

- **Advocate 21st century international literacies** (i.e., the notion that all children must develop the communication skills necessary in an interconnected world, broadening their view of literacy from reading and writing in one language to understanding, presenting information, and conversing in English *and* one or more languages other than English).

- **Develop cross-cultural competency by learning languages** (i.e., the ability to view the world from the perspective of other people and to comfortably function among people of different cultures).

- **Tap into the valuable language resources in our ethnic and indigenous communities.** Heritage-language learners need to maintain and develop high levels of language competency in their first language, and native speakers of English should begin the study of these languages at the elementary level, thereby meeting the need for speakers of languages demanded in the 21st century.

- **Establish a new world language agenda.** Improve world language education in the United States through reforms in teacher training, curriculum and assessment, and the use of technology (Sandrock & Wang, 2005, p. 24–31).

By establishing a new frame for thinking about the value of language learning, and implementing new goals and objectives for language study for all students, we will be able to deliver citizens who are able to communicate and function across linguistic and cultural borders worldwide.

WORKS CITED

American Council on Education. (2002). *Beyond September 11: A comprehensive national policy on international education.* Washington, DC: ACE.

Bales, S. N. (2004, January). *Making the public case for international education: A FrameWorks message memo* (pp. 1–19). Washington, DC: FrameWorks Institute.

Caine, R. N., & Caine, G. (1997). *Education on the edge of possibility.* Alexandria, VA: Association for Supervision and Curriculum Development.

De Mado, J. (1995). *Inclusion in the language classroom* (audiocassette). Washington, CT: John De Mado Language Seminars, Inc.

Donato, R. (1998). Assessing foreign language abilities of the early language learner. In M. Met (Ed.), *Critical issues in early second language learning* (pp. 169–175). Glenview, IL: Scott Foresman-Addison Wesley.

Haas, M. (1998). Early vs. late: The practitioner's perspective. In M. Met (Ed.), *Critical issues in early second language learning* (pp. 43–48). Glenview, IL: Scott Foresman-Addison Wesley.

Hayward, F. M., & Siaya, L. M. (2001). *A report on two national surveys about international education*. Washington, DC: American Council on Education.

Herman, D. M. (2002). "Our patriotic duty": Insights from professional history, 1890–1920. In T. A. Osborn (Ed.), *The future of foreign language in the United States* (pp. 1–23). Westport, CT: Greenwood Publishing Group, Inc.

Hoff-Ginsberg, E. (1998). Is there a critical period for language acquisition? In M. Met (Ed.), *Critical issues in early second language learning* (pp. 31–43). Glenview, IL: Scott Foresman-Addison Wesley.

Huttenlocher, P. R. (1994). Synaptogenesis in human cerebral cortex. In G. Dawson & K. W. Fischer (Eds.), *Human behavior and the developing brain* (pp. 137–152). New York: Guilford Press.

Keatley, C. (2004, March). Who is paying the bills? The federal budget and foreign language education in U.S. schools and universities. *The national language resource newsletter*. Retrieved March 7, 2005, from www.nclrc.org/caidlr82.htm

McColl, H. (2000). *Modern languages for all*. London: David Fulton.

McKeown, S. (2004, August). *Meeting SEN in the curriculum: Modern foreign languages*. London: David Fulton.

Met, M. (2000, Spring). Notes from the president. *Learning Languages, 5*(3), 2–3.

Mok, S. (2004). Address by the Honorable Sam Mok, chief financial officer, U.S. Department of Labor, to the National Language Conference on June 23, 2004, at the University of Maryland.

National Association of State Boards of Education. (2003). The complete curriculum: Ensuring a place for the arts and foreign languages in America's schools. *The report of the NASBE study group on the lost curriculum*. Alexandria, VA: Author.

National Council of State Supervisors for Languages. (2002). *Foreign language education for all students: A position paper*. Retrieved March 3, 2005, from www.ncssfl.org/papers/index.php?allstudents

National Standards in Foreign Language Education Project. (1996). *Standards for foreign language learning: Preparing for the 21st century*. Yonkers, NY: Author.

National Standards in Foreign Language Education Project. (1999). *Standards for foreign language learning in the 21st century*. Lawrence, KS: Allen Press, Inc.

North Carolina Department of Public Instruction. (2003). *The balanced curriculum: A guiding document for scheduling and implementation of the North Carolina standard course of study at the elementary level*. Raleigh, NC: Author.

Sandrock, P., & Wang, S. (2005, March). Building an infrastructure to meet the language needs of all children. *The State Standard*. Alexandria, VA: National Association of State Boards of Education.

Shuler, S. C. (2003, Fall). When no curriculum is left balanced, the needs of children are left behind. *Connecticut Journal of Educational Leadership, 1*, 45–52.

U.S. Department of Defense. (2004). *A call to action for national foreign language capabilities*. Draft white paper. Washington, DC: Author.

U.S. Department of Education, Office of Elementary and Secondary Education. (2001). *No Child Left Behind Act of 2001*. Washington, DC: Author

Von Zastrow, C. (2004, March). *Academic atrophy: The condition of the liberal arts in America's public schools*. Washington, DC: Council for Basic Education.

Wilson, D. R. (2004). *A bibliography of modern foreign languages and special education needs*. Newcastle-upon-Tyne: Author.

Wing, B. H. (Ed.). (1996). *Northeast conference reports—Foreign languages for all: Challenges and choices*. Lincolnwood, IL: National Textbook Company.

II. MAJOR TRENDS AND ISSUES

The field of teaching languages has changed dramatically as a result of world events, research on second-language acquisition, and the standards movement. In this section, we explore in detail how these influences are currently shaping language learning. After an examination of the development of proficiency in students learning new languages, readers will next examine the implications this development has for the teaching of world languages. The key areas influenced by this understanding of second-language acquisition are the instructional environment, curriculum and assessment, program design, and the role of curriculum supervisors. These topics are all discussed with an eye toward what best develops students' proficiency in using a second language.

REALISTIC EXPECTATIONS FOR STUDENTS' SECOND-LANGUAGE PROFICIENCY

In the United States, the field of education has long operated on the belief that two years of study of a language can produce fluent students, and the public has long accepted this as fact. Internationally, however, this has long been known to be false. Research, standards, and performance guidelines tell a different story, describing what students can be expected to do in the language they are learning at key benchmarks, regardless of the grade in which instruction begins. By emphasizing practical communication rather than grammatical analysis in the language-learning classroom, educators are poised to redefine what a language program should deliver.

Learning a language is a lifelong activity. In schools across the United States, native English speakers are required to take English courses from kindergarten through 12th grade. Yet the public, and most students, do not accept that learning another language will take just as long. Those states that require completion of world language classes in order to earn a regular or honors high school diploma have set one, two, or three years of instruction as the requirement. Even English language learners (ELL) are expected to quickly learn their second language, English, in order to exit special ELL classes and enter mainstream courses as soon as possible. However, research on ELL students shows that although the acquisition of a conversational proficiency in English can occur within a few years, the academic proficiency needed to compete with native speakers takes between four and seven years or more to acquire (Thomas & Collier, 1997). And this acquisition is taking place in an environment of immersion in which English is heard, viewed, read, and spoken all day long. This is certainly not the case with world languages. Thus, realistic expectations must be applied to the learning of languages other than English in U.S. schools.

Two documents help classroom teachers establish realistic expectations for what students should be able to do at key points in the development of their proficiency in another language: the communication standards from the national standards document and the ACTFL *Performance Guidelines for K–12 Learners* (American Council on the Teaching of Foreign Languages [ACTFL], 1999). The communication standards establish *what* will be taught; the performance guidelines establish *how well* students will use their new language. The latter are just as important as the former, because without clear targets for how students should be able to perform in the new language, teachers either rely on textbooks to describe language-learning goals or teach vocabulary and grammar without a conscious focus on the language goals students should be able to demonstrate.

The communication standards emphasize treating language learning as more than simply the development of isolated skills (listening, speaking, reading, and writing), encouraging instructors to instead operate on the understanding that the kind of language students can be expected to produce will vary depending on its purpose. For example, beginning language students will speak in an informal conversation between friends with incomplete sentences, occasional mispronunciations, pauses, and the need for the listener to ask for clarification at times. To prepare for speaking in a more formal presentation, however, these same students will take time to organize their thoughts, prepare rough drafts and outlines, revise, and rehearse before presenting a more polished final product. Both forms of speaking are to be expected; it is the purpose behind the communication that helps set a realistic expectation of how well students will use the target language and guides the teacher in establishing what students need to practice in order to succeed.

Three purposes for communication are laid out in the three communication standards (see Figure 1 in the Introduction for a review of the communication standards): interpersonal, interpretive, and presentational. Interpersonal communication is a two-way conversation; it is not memorized dialogues. Interpretive communication is understanding what one reads, hears, or views; it is not translation. Presentational communication is delivering a message in written or spoken form and tailoring it to the intended audience; it is not writing or speaking for the teacher only.

With this framework of the three modes of communication in mind, world language teachers are able to make appropriate decisions about assessment and instruction. Rather than having inflexible rules about allowing students to use bilingual dictionaries, work with partners, or memorize material, such decisions are based on the real-world requirements of each type of communication. Interpersonal conversations are spontaneous, so using a dictionary would only slow down the communication. Instead, students need to practice making themselves understood even without perfect grammar, exact vocabulary, or complete sentences. When doing a presentational writing task, such as a letter to a family abroad that will host a U.S. student on an exchange trip, students want to attend to accuracy and look up the right vocabulary words in order to avoid any miscommunication, because the foreign family members are not present to ask questions of the U.S. student. Expectations for designing the task, as well as for the kind of language students will use in the performance, are completely dependent on the type of communication: interpersonal, interpretive, or presentational. By designing practice tasks and assessments that are based on these real-world communicative purposes, teachers set realistic expectations as to both *how* and *how well* to use the target language.

Does this mean that accuracy never matters? On the contrary, students become more sophisticated in understanding *when* it matters. In situations in which the rules of interpersonal communication reign, if accuracy is lacking, it either won't matter because those conversing will still understand each other, or it will impede understanding and they will work it out—asking questions, restating, clarifying, or using other strategies to be understood and to understand. Students come to know that accuracy is most important in situations requiring presentational communication, because the receiver is not able to engage in such negotiation of meaning. The awareness of audience also increases the need for accuracy in presentational communication.

The second document that has helped to create realistic expectations for student performance is the *ACTFL Performance Guidelines for K–12 Learners* (ACTFL, 1999). (See Appendix.) The motivation for creating these performance guidelines was to put the knowledge gained through oral and written proficiency testing of college-age and adult language learners into a K–12 context. The pathway of increasing proficiency describes the characteristics of language exhibited by K–12 students at three key stages of development, regardless of the age at which they began to learn the language and how they have learned the language. The critical contribution of the performance guidelines is to describe what student language looks like in each of the three modes of communication and at each of three developmental stages: novice, intermediate, and preadvanced. These realistic expectations are based on actual student performance, not simply on what teachers hope to achieve or think they achieve with their classes.

The performance guidelines describe six characteristics of language use:

- Comprehensibility: How well is the student understood?

- Comprehension: How well does the student understand?

- Language Control: How accurate is the student's language?

- Vocabulary: How extensive and applicable is the student's vocabulary?

- Cultural Awareness: How is the student's cultural knowledge reflected in language use?

- Communication Strategies: How does the student maintain communication?

The performance guidelines describe student performance for each of these criteria to illustrate realistic expectations for all three types of communication at the novice, intermediate, and preadvanced levels. These descriptions make clear the pathway that students take as they increase their proficiency in the target language.

The nature of each mode of communication (interpersonal, interpretive, and presentational) necessarily affects these six characteristics of the performance guidelines. Novice-level comprehension in the interpersonal mode, for example, relies on gestures and acting out, as much as on actual words used in order to get one's point across. In contrast, novice-level comprehension in the interpretive mode relies on cognates, those words that are very similar in both one's native language and the language being learned. Cognates are more easily recognized in written form than orally, as cognates often do not sound like their English counterpart. For example, beginning students hearing the Spanish word *nación* usually do not immediately recognize the word until they see it written out, when the similarity with English becomes obvious.

The performance guidelines help teachers know how much to teach at a particular level by basing their instruction on the way students communicate at that level. For example, cultural awareness in the interpersonal mode would be displayed at a novice level as an imitation of the appropriate gestures used when greeting someone; students at a preadvanced level exhibit cultural awareness in the interpersonal mode by using the appropriate idioms to express themselves in a given situation, attending to the culture's requirements in formal or informal settings. The teacher of novice-level students need not spend hours teaching idiomatic expressions, because over time students will learn these as they encounter them in a variety of settings, formal and informal. Instead, the teacher of novice-level students should constantly model the appropriate cultural gestures, knowing that her students will pick them up through observation and repetition. The performance guidelines help teachers set realistic expectations around what should be learned for active use versus what students will learn only for passive recognition. In a grammar-based curriculum, teachers have difficulty identifying how much of a topic to teach. Novice-level learners do not need to know all the intricacies of verb conjugation; rather they may need only to practice communicative exchanges of memorized verbs in the forms they will use to ask, "Do you . . . ?" and to respond, "Yes, I . . . ."

What are realistic expectations for the time it takes to achieve proficiency at the novice, intermediate, and preadvanced levels? Some generalizations can be made in this area based on classroom experiences and oral proficiency interviews conducted with students who began studying their second language in kindergarten, 6th, or 9th grade. Students with instruction of at least three days per week in elementary grades—beginning in 1st grade and continuing with regular instruction through middle and high school—generally perform at the preadvanced level by 12th grade. Students who begin their study of the language in middle school usually achieve the full characteristics of the intermediate level by 12th grade, while also starting to show characteristics of the preadvanced level. Students who begin their study of language in senior high will begin to reach only the intermediate level by 12th grade. An even stronger argument for starting language instruction in elementary grades is not that students acquire traditional grammatical knowledge, but that they gain greater confidence and flexibility in using the target language, especially in interpersonal conversation.

Figure 1 (p. 4) provides a glimpse of what the communication standards and performance guidelines look like in the assessments of a standards-based language classroom, compared to more traditional testing of the four isolated skills of listening, speaking, reading, and writing.

Realistic expectations need to guide all instructional decisions. Teachers, parents, and students must base their expectations for successful language learning on the characteristics of real-world communication and accurate descriptions of the stages through which students progress as they develop increasing proficiency. This is not business as usual. Curricula in world language programs traditionally have been based on a linear grammatical sequence. The 21st century challenge is to create curricula based on how students learn languages and how

they will use them. This holds more challenge than comfort, but ultimately is more rewarding for both students and teachers. By designing assessment through the twin filters of the three modes of communication described in the national standards and the three stages of the performance guidelines, teachers will be able to create effective instructional strategies. The benefit is that students are more motivated to study a world language because they are learning skills that have tangible, real-world applications.

REINVENTING THE INSTRUCTIONAL ENVIRONMENT
Based on realistic expectations for students' developing proficiency in a second language, educators need to look carefully at the instructional environment. The role of the teacher changes dramatically with an understanding of language learning standards and second-language acquisition research. Rather than presenting a linear sequence of grammar concepts and drilling vocabulary items, the standards-based teacher designs meaningful experiences in which students learn the new language by using it for real communication. In this proficiency-oriented instructional environment, the curriculum focuses on cultural perspectives instead of cultural facts and quaint customs. Teachers must redefine the content of language courses by connecting with grade-level curriculum to create engaging contexts for learning.

The Redefined Role of Content in Language Learning
The content of the world language classroom goes beyond linguistic content and integrates all student learning into instruction that provides a broader range of meaningful, engaging, and authentic language-learning experiences. Content

■ Represents important topics and ideas that help students understand the world in which they live and who they are, and

■ Helps students respond to important questions that extend learning beyond the classroom (Clementi, 2004).

According to Genesee and Cloud (1998), "students develop advanced levels of language competency most successfully when they are engaged in meaningful and challenging communication about non-language subjects" (p. 64). The use of content in the world languages classroom is also strongly supported by both second-language acquisition theory and brain research. In Stephen Krashen's comprehensible input theory of second-language acquisition (1982), language is best acquired when

■ The focus of instruction is on meaning rather than form;

■ Language input is at or just above the proficiency of the learner; and

■ Sufficient opportunity exists to engage in meaningful language use in a relatively anxiety-free environment.

Curtain (1995) emphasizes that comprehensible input best occurs when children are active learners of cognitively challenging curricula. Furthermore, studies by cognitive psychologists confirm that information is best stored in the brain when it is meaningful to students (Caine & Caine, 1997; Sprenger, 1999; Wolfe, 2001), and that meaningfulness always occurs in a context-rich environment.

The efficacy of using content from other areas of the school curriculum is emphasized in the national standards and in many state standards documents. The *connections* goal in the national standards includes two standards (3.1 and 3.2); the first focuses on student reinforcement and furthering of their knowledge of other disciplines through foreign language, and the second focuses on student acquisition of knowledge and recognition of distinctive viewpoints that are only available through a foreign

language and its culture (National Standards in Foreign Language Education Project, 1999). The use of content in the world language classroom thereby supports the concept of communicative- and standards-based language instruction in that it provides a meaningful context for language use. Students acquire new language structures and patterns through interesting and relevant topics that provide opportunities for extended discourse. Curtain and Dahlberg (2004) summarize the benefits of using content from other curricular areas in language instruction

■ To integrate language development with content learning.

■ To provide a vehicle for reinforcing the academic skills and processes and the cognitive skills required by the regular curriculum.

■ To enrich concepts learned in other content areas with the unique experiences and insights available through language study. (p. 249)

The community section of the national standards further emphasizes student application of content learned *through the language* in real-world situations in the language classroom, in their local communities, and beyond. The community standards encourage teachers to design meaningful learning experiences outside the classroom that may involve multistep, experiential projects that end in the completion of a real-world task or product, as seen in the GLOBE (Global Learning and Observations to Benefit the Environment) program. GLOBE is a cooperative effort of schools that is led in the United States by a federal interagency program supported by NASA, the National Science Foundation, and the U.S. State Department, in partnership with colleges and universities, state and local school systems, and nongovernment organizations. Internationally, GLOBE represents a partnership between the United States and more than 100 other countries.

The GLOBE program provides an excellent means for language teachers to integrate science—and other subjects such as mathematics, technology, and social studies—into their instruction (Kennedy, 1999; Kennedy & Canney, 2000). GLOBE participants include students from more than 100 countries who monitor atmospheric, hydrologic, geologic, and biometric conditions in their local communities and make comparisons with other schools around the world. They report their data via the Internet to the GLOBE network and through periodic Web chats in participating countries. These chats provide opportunities for spontaneous communication in the target language, helping students improve their conversational skills. One recent discussion centered on El Niño and its effects, particularly in Central America. Students from many different schools in both South America and the United States participated. Many different dialects of Spanish were used, exposing students to a broad learning community (Kennedy, 2003). The GLOBE program can bring virtually every classroom in a school together to work on a single project with other students and scientists on an international level. Although GLOBE's primary focus is science, it also provides students of a second language with authentic opportunities to communicate in the language they are studying. Science serves as a focal point around which oral language and literacy can develop (Kennedy, 1999).

What does the language classroom look like when content is the organizing principle of instruction? Various prototype program models exist for how content can be integrated into language instruction. In the *total immersion* model, time is spent learning subject matter taught in the foreign language, and language learning per se is systematically integrated throughout the curriculum. The *partial immersion* approach differs in that only 50

percent of the day is conducted in the target language. In *two-way immersion* or *dual language* programs, the student population consists of English-dominant speakers and heritage speakers of a specific language. Subject content and language skills are taught 50 percent of the time in the heritage language and 50 percent in English. The goals of the two-way or dual models include functional proficiency in the second language on age-appropriate topics, learning subject content from the general curriculum, and cross-cultural understanding and achievement in English language arts that is comparable to or surpasses the achievement of students in English-only programs (Curtain & Pesola, 1994). In *content-based* instruction, the foreign language teacher assumes responsibility for teaching certain areas of the grade-level curriculum. In *content-related* or *content-enriched* instruction, one of the most commonly found models in elementary and middle school programs, the foreign language teacher uses concepts from the general curriculum to enrich language instruction with academic content.

Concepts from content areas such as social studies, mathematics, science, and language arts provide a natural link to language instruction. Social studies topics dealing with the home, family, community, social patterns, and comparative cultures mirror the same topics taught in language programs. Mathematics concepts involving computation, statistics, measurement, and concrete problem solving are easily communicated and transferred in second-language instruction. Hands-on activities conducted in science provide an excellent opportunity for meaningful student interaction in the second language (Curtain & Dahlberg, 2004). Language arts literacy topics also can be integrated into second-language instruction, with the added value of reinforcing literacy skills. Through the study of age-appropriate children's literature, students can identify the main idea and supporting details, search for key vocabulary terms related to a theme, and guess the meaning of unknown words from context. The incorporation of the writing process in the second language strengthens students' ability to organize thoughts and support opinions.

Thematic units or *learning scenarios* are terms currently used to describe extended units of study organized around a particular theme. In addition to incorporating content from other disciplines, extended thematic units

■ Incorporate the *Standards for Foreign Language Learning in the 21st Century* (National Standards Foreign Language Education Project, 1999) by allowing students to develop the interpersonal, interpretive, and presentational modes of communication; compare and contrast the native and target languages and cultures; gather and share information from the point of view of both the native and target cultures; and connect learners to a language community in a real or virtual manner.

■ Are of high interest and are age- and level-appropriate.

■ Incorporate authentic target language materials and the use of technology.

■ Promote the development of critical-thinking skills.

■ Involve learners in the development of a final product of their choice, using the target language to conduct research and gain new knowledge about their own and other cultures.

■ Allow students to begin to see the purpose of language study as something with real-world value and lifelong advantages. (Spinelli & Nerenz, 2004, p. 3)

Good thematic teaching captures students' imaginations, is perceived as important to teachers and learners, legitimizes the disciplinary content

that is integrated into instruction, accommodates a variety of learning approaches, and has the added value of increased student motivation and an improved attitude toward learning.

The following examples are taken from the learning scenarios in the *Standards for Foreign Language Learning in the 21st Century* (National Standards in Foreign Language Education Project, 1999).

Example 1: Butterflies (novice level)

The scenario below has been developed for use in an elementary setting, but also can be adapted for use at the middle and high school levels with appropriate modifications.

Students at Sanchez Elementary School are fascinated by the yearly migration of butterflies. Their interest is channeled into an expansive interdisciplinary learning project. The art teacher helps them make butterflies from origami and tissue paper. In language arts, students research and write a report on the butterfly. Social studies classes color maps showing the flight path of the monarch butterfly, while math teachers have students construct butterfly shapes to study symmetry. Students in science learn about the life cycle of a butterfly. The theme even extends to health and physical education, where Coach Garcia teaches his students how to do the butterfly stroke and how to use a butterfly bandage.

Senorita Rodriguez teaches her students the names for the various parts of the butterfly in Spanish, using samples provided by the art teacher. Students point to the different colors as she calls them out in the target language. Students may also show and tell about butterflies by using familiar adjectives to describe them and by identifying the six stages of their life cycle. Working in pairs, students use cardinal numbers to trace the migration of the monarch butterfly on a map, as well as to provide information regarding shape, color, size, and symmetry. Working in cooperative groups, students are asked to compose a verse about the butterfly. The project culminates with a field trip to a local museum of natural science to observe butterflies in their natural habitat. (p. 73)

Reflection

Standard 1.1 (Communication) Students use the language to identify parts of the butterfly and answer questions.

Standard 1.3 (Communication) Students talk about butterflies and compose a verse about them.

Standard 3.1 (Connections) Students further their knowledge of butterflies in an interdisciplinary fashion.

This is an example of an integrated curriculum in which each subject seeks to provide learning opportunities for students around a common theme. The learning throughout the day is then reinforced for students not only through different disciplines but also through different learning modalities. This interdisciplinary aspect is particularly pertinent to language learning because students make connections among disciplines and see an immediate use and application for the other language. This approach is most easily accomplished in the elementary school setting, but it can be used effectively at the middle and high school levels with appropriate planning.

Example 2: *Damals war es Friedrich* (intermediate level)

The scenario below revolves around a thematic unit based on a novel by Hans Peter Richter.

The students in the fourth-year German course at Las Cruces High School, N.M., have spent the past three weeks reading *Damals war es Friedrich*, a novel by Hans Peter Richter that focuses on the relationship between Jewish and non-Jewish boys growing up during the 1930s. While reading, the students discuss various literary aspects of the novel, including its structure and relationship to other literary works that they have read; the relationships of the characters to each other; and the historical setting of the novel. The nine students decide in a brainstorming session to produce a "documentary" film based on the historical period depicted in the novel and focused on the period's effect on families. Students plan to contact history teachers in the school, professors in the German and history departments at the local university, Jewish community leaders, and the leadership of *Freude der deutschen Sprache*, a community organization for German speakers. Some students videotape interviews with members of the community who lived in Germany during that time period. Other students write scripts for scenes from the book, emphasizing the Jewish boy's perspective. The group tapes these scenes, with members of the class taking on various roles. Still other students do historical research. One student's inquiries lead to the discovery of a Holocaust museum in a neighboring city, which the class visits. The students interview the museum's founder and director and capture many of the displays on videotape. The group also views several films, including *Europa, Europa*; *Die Weisse Rose (The White Rose)*; *Schindler's List*; and parts of a documentary film on *entartete kunst* (degenerate art) and filmmaker Leni Riefenstahl. Using two VCRs, the students edit the scenes they filmed, including relevant parts of the interviews and footage from the museum visit. Finally, they add introductory and closing comments and voice-over narration by some of the students. The finished film, a copy of which is sent to the museum for its archives, is about 25 minutes long and is augmented by a written synopsis of the project. (pp. 273–4)

Reflection

Standard 1.1 (Communication) Students brainstorm and plan their project using the language. Students interview community leaders.

Standard 1.2 (Communication) Students read a novel, view a film, and research a project using secondary sources. Students produce a film and synopsis.

Standard 2.1 (Culture) Students discover through their reading, viewing, and research how the historical period was presented in the culture.

Standard 2.2 (Culture) Students view films produced by the culture studied.

Standard 3.1 (Connections) Students further their knowledge of the period.

Standard 3.2 (Connections) Students find perspectives that differ from those presented in their history textbooks.

Standard 4.1 (Comparisons) In viewing a film, students comment on the difference between the spoken dialogue and subtitles.

Standard 5.1 (Communities) Students use the community as a resource.

Standard 5.2 (Communities) Students research a topic using resources other than print material.

This scenario illustrates how a literary work can serve as the basis for an interdisciplinary project. Even though this community does not have a large number of native speakers, the students were able to locate speakers of the language who could contribute to their project. A logical extension of this project would be to broadcast the video on a local cable or university channel for the community to see, or to host a screening attended by those who were interviewed. The final product in this scenario

also could have been a print publication of some variety.

The Redefined Role of Culture in Language Learning

In the prestandards world language classroom, the teaching of culture typically focused on providing students with factual information about various customs, traditions, holidays, artifacts, music, art, or historical events of the language studied. Textbooks addressed it in sidebar sections of each chapter that contained randomly selected pieces of information on isolated aspects of a given culture. Culture was identified as the "fifth skill" in the hierarchy of skills in the language classroom, which both reinforced the idea that it was not the most important component of language learning and proliferated the notion of a natural separation between language and culture. Teachers routinely selected certain aspects of the culture they wished to emphasize at each level of instruction and assessed student cultural knowledge through discrete point quizzes and unit tests, with minimal points assigned to the "culture section." Such a superficial approach illustrates how culture often has been included as an afterthought in the language curriculum, resulting in marginal or negligible student outcomes in this area.

How has the teaching of culture changed since the creation of national standards? A 1999 study of 12,000 high school teachers conducted by the Social Science Education Consortium reports that although foreign language teachers maintain support for the teaching of culture and perceive they are incorporating culture into instruction, this is not reflected in their actual teaching. Currently, almost a decade since the release of the 1996 standards, an informal electronic survey of members of the National Council of State Supervisors for Languages (September 11, 2004) shows that the continuous and systematic integration of culture is *sometimes* found in language instruction (Jensen, 2004). Additionally, supervisors *somewhat agree* that one-way transmission of facts still is the most common means of teaching culture in the classroom, indicating that only marginal progress has been made in how culture is taught since the release of the standards. One factor that may be contributing to the lack of greater progress in this area is the dearth of adequate preservice and inservice training on both the teaching of culture and the process of cross-cultural inquiry that leads to the development of cross-cultural awareness.

Students do not acquire cultural awareness on their own. Galloway (1999) emphasizes the need to reframe the teaching of language and culture with the goal of "growing the cross-cultural mind" (p. 153). She maintains that teachers need to prepare students for culture learning by facilitating their understanding of what it means to be a product of a culture. This happens by first helping students recognize their own culture-based values and attitudes. Students need to discover that they have a culture before they can recognize and become open to other frames of reference. Once this realization occurs, all language learning activities should be embedded in a cultural context that reflects the "real world" of language.

Unless teachers are provided with the tools to deliver this type of instruction in the language classroom, the teaching of culture will not change. The time has come for the field to refocus on the standards as the foundation of a new vision of cross-cultural education. It is not by accident that culture is infused in all of the standards (Communication, Cultures, Connections, Comparisons, and Communities) and in all topics related to communication. Within each of these goals, culture dominates as an integral and recurring strand. The continuous, systematic integration of culture is essential to the teaching and learning of languages.

Language and culture are, in reality, one and the same and are mutually dependent in the underlying culture. Most linguists agree that language is reflective of and influenced by the culture in which it is found. Teaching language *is* teaching culture and teaching culture *is* teaching language, because communication is the ability to use language in culturally sensitive ways. According to Galloway, the goals of language instruction can best be stated as teaching culture through the tools of its languages. She underscores the need for a new *culture* agenda: "A language agenda where culture never fits will be exchanged for a culture agenda where language is the currency" (Galloway, 1999, p. 156).

To understand how language *and* culture learning become an everyday occurrence in the world language classroom requires taking a look at the anthropological approach to conceptualizing culture found in the standards—understanding culture within the context of the *products*, social *practices*, and philosophical *perspectives* of a society. The culture standard in the national standards focuses on how cultural products and practices reflect perspectives (attitudes, values, and beliefs of the culture) as well as how products and practices interact to change perspectives. Based on the premise that language is culture, the modes of communication in the standards provide a natural and complimentary means to organize the teaching of culture into the curriculum.

The communications standards support the belief that culture is an integral part of all language use and is learned not just by talking about it, but by experiencing it through using the language. For example, in the presentational mode, beginning-level students might reproduce expressive products of the target culture and describe them using simple language; more advanced students might present the results of research showing how expressive products or innovations of the target culture influence the global community. In the interpersonal mode, beginning students might participate in a variety of oral and written activities after listening to or reading age-appropriate, culturally authentic selections, whereas more advanced students might demonstrate and discuss certain observable patterns of behavior and social conventions of the target culture peer group and make comparisons with those in the United States. Moreover, given the direct link between assessment and instruction, these instructional activities become the very authentic performance tasks that enable students to demonstrate their understanding of the products, practices, and perspectives of a culture through the modes of communication.

Allen (1999) makes a strong case for the efficacy of the backward design curriculum model (Wiggins & McTighe, 1998) in standards-based foreign language instruction by illustrating how culture is easily and consistently integrated with language learning. In step one of the five-step backward design approach, culture and language are integrated by specifying both cultural and language achievement targets. In the second step, language is further integrated with culture by developing an assessment task that models real communication in authentic contexts and requires students to engage in interpersonal, interpretive, or presentational communication. In step three, both cultural and linguistic student objectives are determined by specifying enabling knowledge and skills. In the fourth step, cultural activities designed to lead students to a meaningful understanding of culture are integrated with language activities designed to lead students to the effective performance of the assessment task. The fifth step ensures students are able to provide evidence that they have met both the cultural and linguistic objectives through a process of trial and error in light of teacher feedback (Allen, 1999, p. 17). The litmus test to determine whether culture is systematically included in the language curriculum lies in the answer to this question: Are instructional and assessment activities that lead students to a meaningful understanding of culture consistently integrated into daily practice through authentic interpersonal, interpretive, and presentational communication tasks?

The Redefined Role of the Teacher in Language Learning

The new framework for the teaching and learning of other languages and culture found in the *Standards for Foreign Language Learning* (1996, 1999) has had a profound effect on the role of the teacher. The student standards emphasize the contexts in which communication takes place and require the hiring and retention of teachers with higher levels of competence in language use and cultural knowledge than in the past. Teachers also must possess new pedagogical knowledge and skills in order to implement the more challenging performance-based model of language instruction and assessment—a model that requires instructional activities and assessments to provide students with opportunities to use *and* create personal meaning with language in a wide range of contexts, as encountered in the target culture. Additionally, teachers must have an understanding of current theories that underline new instructional approaches for diverse learners and a solid grounding in the use of technology. This represents a dramatic shift from the knowledge and skills needed to meet the goals of the traditional, linguistics-based language classroom and necessitates rethinking teaching approaches to enable students to meet the standards. The good news is that the development of national standards that define the *what* of language learning and the *ACTFL K–12 Performance Guidelines* (1999) that define the *how well* of language learning, coupled with recent cognitive research, have provided teachers with new tools to foster change. This has caused a shift in focus from teaching to *learning* and has brought along exciting and innovative reconceptualizations of how best to help students learn.

In *Characteristics of Effective Foreign Language Instruction*, the National Association of District

Supervisors of Foreign Languages (NADSFL) (1999) outlines characteristics that reflect the national standards and focus on student learning. The list was compiled on the basis of language acquisition theory and research and is grounded in district supervisors' collective experience as classroom practitioners and teacher observers. These characteristics are remarkably similar to the *Key Concepts for Success: Elementary and Middle School Foreign Languages* outlined by nationally recognized K–8 teacher educators Helena Curtain and Carol Ann Dahlberg (2004, p. xiv), perhaps unsurprising given that they support teaching strategies that lead to student achievement of the standards.

Figure 2 illustrates the link to many of the key concepts and goals outlined in the national student standards and the effective teaching approaches suggested by NADSFL and Curtain and Dahlberg. It is important to note that even though the *Key Concepts for Success* are geared toward elementary and middle school teaching, they are highly applicable for the secondary level as well.

In their redefined roles as facilitators in student-centered world language classrooms, teachers constantly are revising and refining teaching strategies, materials, and activities to meet the needs and interests of all students. Teachers empower learners with this flexibility in instruction, enabling all students to attain the goal of communicative-based language instruction—namely, preparing for authentic language use in the real world. The essential question for teachers to consider in their redefined roles in the second-language classroom is this: What kinds of opportunities can I create and skillfully facilitate in my classes to ensure all students have an opportunity to be successful language and culture learners? Figure 3 provides an example of the communicative approach to world language instruction.

DESIGNING CURRICULUM VIA ASSESSMENT TARGETS

Starting with the benchmarks for developing proficiency in a second language, teachers and supervisors design an effective curriculum by capturing the targeted student performance in unit-level assessments. This backward design is critical to moving language teaching away from the linear sequence of vocabulary and grammar. Using lessons learned from second-language acquisition research, teachers are better able to design curriculum that identifies what knowledge and skills students need to accomplish a specific communicative task, rather than listing an entire grammar topic and leaving the teacher to find a meaningful use for it. In addition, students practice these communication skills in a thematic context that is meaningful, engaging, and cognitively challenging. The key for curriculum is to identify appropriate measures to assess students' developing proficiency.

Planning Curriculum

Planning curriculum provides teachers an opportunity to look more closely at what they are teaching and identify the real goals for their instruction. Teachers reveal the actual curriculum they are teaching when they identify the focus of the day's lesson or their current unit. Comparing a teacher's reflection on what is being taught with the planned or written curriculum gives the teacher, administrator, content supervisor, parent, and student an insight into the true focus of the daily and unit-level planning.

Teachers of languages have been on a curriculum journey for the past 20 years or more, a journey that has dramatically affected how they answer the question, "What are you teaching?" In the prestandards world language classroom, many teachers created curriculum simply by writing down the table of contents from the selected textbook. The topics for instruction were a linear sequence of grammar points and topical vocabulary. When asked what they were teaching, world language teachers might respond with the grammar item of the

Figure 2
Comparison of Key Concepts and Goals

Standards for Foreign Language Learning in the 21st Century (National Standards in Foreign Language Education Project, 1999)	*Characteristics of Effective Foreign Language Instruction* (NADSFL, 1999)	*Key Concepts for Success: Elementary and Middle School Foreign Languages* (Curtain & Dahlberg, 2004)
All Students		
"All children are primed to learn languages, and they will rise to meet expectations when goals are appropriately set and the conditions for learning are designed to foster achievement" (p. 24).	—The teacher sets high expectations for *all* students and designs assessments and instruction to engage and motivate *all* learners. —*All* students are guided to use all levels of thinking skills, e.g., they repeat, recognize, and recall as well as apply, create, and predict. —The diverse learning styles of *all* students are considered in teaching and instructional planning.	—Activities are geared to the young learner's interests, cognitive level, motor skills level, and experiential background. They are designed to appeal to a variety of learning styles, to address multiple intelligences, and to incorporate frequent opportunities for physical activity.
Meaningful Communication		
"Meaningful language from real contexts becomes the basis for subsequent development of expressive skills" (p. 39). "It is essential that learners be surrounded with interesting and age-appropriate materials as a basis for acquisition of a new language system in its cultural contexts" (p. 39).	—The teacher and students communicate purposefully in the target language as listeners, speakers, readers, writers, and viewers.	—Learning occurs in meaningful communicative contexts that carry significance for the student. For the young learner, these contexts include social and cultural situations, subject content instruction, and experiences with activities such as art, crafts, sports, and hobbies. —Learners are surrounded by meaningful language, both oral and written, from beginning through advanced stages of language acquisition. —Teachers consistently conduct instruction in the target language with minimal use of the native language. The target language and the native language are kept distinctly separate.

Figure 2 (*continued*)
Comparison of Key Concepts and Goals

Standards for Foreign Language Learning in the 21st Century (National Standards in Foreign Language Education Project, 1999)	*Characteristics of Effective Foreign Language Instruction* (NADSFL, 1999)	*Key Concepts for Success: Elementary and Middle School Foreign Languages* (Curtain & Dahlberg, 2004)
Student-Centered Approach		
"Active use of language is central to the learning process. [Students] learn by doing, by trying out language, and by modifying it to serve communicative needs" (p. 41). "Students should be given ample opportunities to explore, develop, and use communication strategies, learning strategies, critical thinking skills, and skills in technology, as well as the appropriate elements of the language system and culture" (p. 32).	—Lessons contain more student activity than teacher activity. This includes student-to-student interactions as well as teacher-to-student interactions. Students work independently, in pairs, and in groups. Students ask and answer questions that they create with the target language. —Students take risks as language learners because the learning environment is positive and supportive. —Students use language-specific learning strategies and are encouraged to assess their own progress.	—Teachers recognize learners as active constructors of meaning rather than passive receivers of vocabulary and information. They scaffold instruction so that learners become increasingly independent in their use of the spoken and written target language. —Learners use their growing awareness of language and language learning strategies to gain increasing independence and self-direction as learners.
Organization of Instruction		
"Knowledge of a second language and culture combines with the study of other disciplines and shifts the focus from language acquisition to broader learning experiences for the student" (p. 53). "Students must be given interesting and challenging topics and ideas that they can read about, discuss, or analyze" (p. 35).	—Students and teachers are not text-bound during instructional time. It is obvious that the text is a tool, not the curriculum. —Students and teachers use a variety of print and nonprint materials, including authentic target language resources. —Students and teachers use technology, as available, to facilitate learning and teaching.	—The foreign language program draws from and reinforces the goals of the general curriculum, including across-the-curriculum goals such as cognitive skills development and global education. —Planning is organized around a thematic center and aligned with content and performance standards. Attention is paid to achieving balance among the basic goals of culture, subject content, and language use.
Culture		
"The study of language provides opportunities for students to develop insights into a culture that are available in no other way. In reality, then, the true content of the foreign language course is not the grammar and vocabulary of the language, but the cultures expressed through that language" (pp. 47–48).	—Culture is a natural component of language use in all activities. —Students have positive attitudes toward cultural diversity that are demonstrated in the learning environment.	—Culture is learned through experiences with cultural materials and practices. Elements from the target language's culture are essential components of all planning and teaching.

Figure 2 (*continued*)
Comparison of Key Concepts and Goals

Standards for Foreign Language Learning in the 21st Century (National Standards in Foreign Language Education Project, 1999)	*Characteristics of Effective Foreign Language Instruction* (NADSFL, 1999)	*Key Concepts for Success: Elementary and Middle School Foreign Languages* (Curtain & Dahlberg, 2004)
Assessment		
"Standards preparation is forcing attention to the broader view of second-language study and competence: What should students know and be able to do—and how well?" (p. 15)	Assessments are ongoing. Students are assessed formally and informally on how well they are able to meet the objectives of the lesson. Continuous self-assessments for students and teachers are encouraged.	Assessment of learning is frequent, regular, and ongoing in a manner that is consistent with targeted standards, program goals, and teaching strategies.

week—such as *-ar* verbs or passé composé—and the vocabulary topic, which might be colors, food, or shopping. With such discrete items as the focus for instruction, the daily lesson plan centered on drills and practice activities to teach the grammar concepts and vocabulary of the unit.

The challenge inherent in using grammar and vocabulary to organize the curriculum is the lack of any indication of how much of each item to teach. How much knowledge of stem-changing verbs is needed for beginning students? How much drilling of irregular verb forms is needed? How many body parts need to be memorized? What furniture items should be taught? How much about various structures do students need to know in their first, third, or fifth year of instruction? Without clear goals for students' language performance, teachers designed instruction in which students learned about the target language through a set sequence of grammar topics. This approach to curriculum planning emphasized the activities of teaching rather than students' acquisition of language.

The standards-based mindset for curriculum planning has had a profound effect on teachers' instructional decisions. The focus has shifted from what the teacher does—building repertoire to teach and test discrete items—to what the students do—

building their skills in using a new language. Teachers in the standards era must first identify the end goals of instruction. This clear target then becomes a filter through which the teacher is better able to make the myriad instructional decisions faced every day. Rather than seeking better ways to teach grammar and vocabulary and then assessing students' achievement, teachers in world language classrooms must focus on what and how students actually are learning, frequently checking students' progress toward the targeted performance.

For learning languages, the implication is clear: the curriculum is a spiral, with topics frequently reentering and content regularly revisited. The world language teacher does not merely teach a particular verb form, but the applications of that verb form students will need in order to successfully perform the unit's end task. Today's world language teacher will not try to teach all six forms of a verb if that unit's final performance is simply to ask a friend questions and answer for oneself, requiring only the "you" and "I" forms of the verb. The teacher will decide when to teach the remaining forms depending on when, or whether, such information will be necessary for an assessment task. The world language teacher will no longer teach grammar and vocabulary simply because it is on a list or in a

---

Figure 3
The Communicative Approach—An Illustrative Example

Goals: To become communicatively competent, able to use language appropriate for a given social context; to manage the process of negotiating meaning with interlocutors.

Roles: Teacher facilitates students' learning by managing classroom activities, setting up communicative situations. Students are communicators, actively engaged in negotiating meaning.

Teaching and Learning Process: Activities are communicative—they represent an information gap that needs to be filled; speakers have a choice of what to say and how to say it; they receive feedback from the listener that will verify that a purpose has been achieved; authentic materials are used. Students usually work in small groups.

Interaction: Student-Teacher and Student-Student: Teacher initiates interactions between students and sometimes participates. Students interact a great deal with each other in many configurations.

Dealing with Feelings: Emphasis is on developing motivation to learn through establishing meaningful, purposeful things to do with the target language. Individuality is encouraged as well as cooperation with peers, which both contribute to a sense of emotional security with the target language.

View of Language and Culture: Language is for communication. Linguistic competence must be coupled with an ability to convey intended meaning appropriately in different social contexts. Culture is the everyday life of native speakers of the target language. Nonverbal behavior is important.

Aspects of Language the Approach Emphasizes: Functions are emphasized over forms, with simple forms learned for each function before more complex forms. Students work at discourse level. They work on speaking, listening, reading, and writing from the beginning. Consistent focus is placed on negotiated meaning.

Role of Students' Native Language: Students' native language usually plays no role.

Means for Evaluation: Informal evaluation takes place when the teacher advises or communicates; formal evaluation is by means of an integrative test with a real communicative function.

Response to Student Errors: Errors of form are considered natural; students with incomplete knowledge still can succeed as communicators.

Source: From "Eight Approaches to Language Teaching," by G. Doggett, 2003, *CAL Digest Series 1: Complete Collection*, p. 168. Washington, DC: Center for Applied Linguistics. Copyright 2003 by the Center for Applied Linguistics. Reprinted with permission.

textbook chapter, but rather will teach exactly what students will need for a very purposeful and meaningful performance. By starting with the actual student performance goal for the unit, the teacher knows how much of the grammar or vocabulary items students need to learn. With this type of curriculum and planning, all instruction works efficiently toward the true end goal.

Lessons from English Language Learners

At about the same time that the performance assessment and standards movements were coming into the consciousness of world language teachers, new waves of immigrant students were arriving in U.S. schools. State education agencies and local school districts quickly mobilized to train the English as a second language (ESL) teachers needed to meet these new demands. ESL teachers faced the urgent need to help students of all ages quickly learn English in order to join their English-speaking classmates in academic subjects. Lacking a common language among students for instruction, these teachers were not able to teach English by explaining its grammatical structures in the students' native languages. ESL teachers used immersion techniques that provided students with many different ways to comprehend written and spoken messages. These teachers had to use English to teach math, science, social studies, physical education, and art, too. Students proved how well they were learning to use English by completing meaningful assignments in those subject areas, not abstract worksheets manipulating grammatical concepts. These teaching techniques reflected the real-life applications students faced on a daily basis.

Teachers of languages other than English paid attention. They watched the way ESL teachers were teaching and how quickly students learned to use their new language. The dramatic results proved to world language teachers that they could trust immersion techniques and reinforced many of their beliefs about language acquisition. These experiences taught language educators to be mindful of when and how students will actually use the target language and to let real-life applications guide instructional decisions and motivate students.

Although many similarities exist between the language learning of immigrant students studying English in the United States and native speakers of English learning other languages, teachers also must be attentive to some differences. For instance, each group learns the new language based on a different need: ESL students feel intense pressure to master English quickly, including survival, social, and academic language, whereas native English-speaking students are less dependent on acquiring a second language for their future success. Yes, languages will open doors and unlock new possibilities for all students, but most U.S. students won't rely on the language they are studying for survival or academic purposes; instead, it will be useful in their futures for career advantages, for the exchange and acquisition of information, and for the depth of cultural understanding it brings.

If they lack the urgency of ESL students in learning a second language, U.S. students learning languages other than English in grades K–12 do bring background knowledge from learning in their first language. They know how to learn and read, and can make comparisons with their own language and culture, especially beyond the primary grades.

In addition, adolescent students are entering a more analytical phase of their learning and can speed up their acquisition of a second language by understanding how it works, rather than just intuitively coming to conclusions.

The lesson American educators have learned in teaching English and other languages to students in U.S. schools is that planning curriculum must be based on specific end goals. Teachers need to create curriculum that focuses on practical and realistic performance targets. Such targets must consider what students can do with their new language, not what they can say about it. Being realistic in determining what students can do in the target language means that teachers cannot simply assume that students have full control of everything that has been taught; rather, they need to understand the process of language learning, which moves from exposure to the language, to some ability to manipulate grammatical structures, to some spontaneous use of these concepts and, finally, to full control. The true goal for a unit needs to be stated in terms of the functional use and application of the language learned. When such end goals are clear from the start, they motivate students and the teacher. The teacher faces clear—and, thus, easier—instructional decisions in her daily and unit planning. She has a learning target to help frame answers to questions such as how much is needed of any specific vocabulary or grammar item or which language functions need to be emphasized. Where previously they had no reliable source for making such decisions, teachers now can look to the end performance to guide all instruction and assessment.

Redefining the Thematic Context for Language Learning

If a clearly described performance in the target language is the curriculum goal for each unit of instruction, then what is the context for language learning? This is the next decision to guide a teacher's daily and unit planning. As previously described, world language teachers have been on a journey toward a more real-world application of the knowledge and skills students learn in their classrooms. In the traditional language classroom, contexts centered on vocabulary topics as teachers developed units on family, school, housing, pastimes, holidays, and capital cities. In today's learning environment, world language teachers must identify the purpose behind studying such topics. The thematic focus of a unit of instruction must provide a deeper exploration and a richer context beyond mere vocabulary. Conscious of the need for a meaningful context for learning, teachers might now extend their housing unit beyond the names of rooms and furnishings to, perhaps, using Venn diagrams to explore common and unique characteristics of housing in both cultures.

To illustrate this shift in context, consider the traditional unit that focuses on family. Students certainly need to learn the words for various relatives and some descriptive words, but for what purpose? The end goal no longer is simply to pass a spelling quiz on the words for family members or to label a family tree. Nor is the unit limited just to families in countries where the target language is spoken. Instead, the unit's context expands to explore the concept of family and differences within a wider variety of cultures. The unit's activities should be guided by important questions for students to explore, such as: Do grandparents live with the nuclear family? Do children stay at home or nearby as they reach adulthood? What responsibilities do children have at home in various cultures? The teacher determines the appropriateness of such questions based on the age of the students and their areas of interest. Beginning students, for example, will use simple language to list similarities and differences of families in different cultures. Although students still may do some of the traditional activities, such as labeling a family tree, the end goal is

something richer and deeper: helping students to understand cultural similarities and differences.

Another common unit at the beginning level of language study is numbers and colors. When teachers try to identify the end goal for such instruction, they begin to understand that such topics do not make up a unit. Numbers and colors are not the end in and of themselves; instead, they are tools to get to a deeper understanding of another topic. A potential application for numbers and colors lies within a unit on the arts as a means of expression. Now numbers and colors are important as tools to talk about works of art. Even at beginning levels, students might start with concrete descriptors such as the number of objects, colors, or emotions they see in the artwork. They then might move on to identify the style, the event, or the cultural phenomenon reflected in the work by offering a simple description of it. Finally, they might use vocabulary and structures to discuss their likes and dislikes regarding works of art while doing a gallery walk in small groups.

This broader context for a thematic unit also includes a cultural overlay on several levels. At its most basic, the cultural overlay reminds the teacher to share the connotations of words that cannot easily be translated from one language to another. For example, the English word *friends* can be translated in French into *copains* and *amies*. However, it is critical to know that *amies* is used to refer to very close friends and *copains* is closer to the English *acquaintances*. The use of each word in its correct cultural connotation might be practiced in the classroom with simulation activities. On another level, the unit's cultural overlay leads the teacher to describe practices, such as who lives in the house: Grandparents? Children who have graduated from the university? Or how rooms are used: Where does the family generally watch TV? Where do children study? The cultural products related to the thematic unit are another consideration. An example might include students using the layout of a city map to explore whether people walk or drive around the community to go shopping or to school; whether public transportation is feasible and, if so, what types exist; and what opportunities exist for social outings when students don't drive. Students can compare these findings to their own community. In identifying what is common in their community, students learn the valuable lesson that they should not overgeneralize findings but instead consider qualifying information, such as how many people are in a particular category or how something varies at different times or for different ages. Students quickly learn in such cultural explorations to avoid saying "all" and to start saying "some."

From explorations of these factual components of a cultural topic, students also begin to develop an understanding of differences in perspectives among cultures. For example, students will better understand a culture's attitude toward conservation when they relate that attitude to the physical geography or city layout common in that culture. This is the type of focus on a theme that carries learning far beyond mere vocabulary. Such depth helps teachers design instructional units that will engage and motivate students.

Creating a New Context for Assessment

If world language educators think back to how they traditionally have designed curriculum and instruction, they probably will describe the process of identifying a grammar concept and then searching for a thematic topic within which students would logically use the grammar. Unfortunately, what they ended up with was simply grammar in a cultural wrapping. For example, if they wanted to teach command forms, they might have assumed that a unit on shopping or travel would give students a chance to practice giving commands as they ask for directions on how to find different stores. But even though students may need

commands in order to give directions, they don't need to learn the grammatical concept of command forms to be successful at it. Students could more quickly learn as vocabulary items the three or four commands needed for giving directions, for example, turn left/right, go straight ahead for two blocks, on your left/right, cross the street. Rather than framing the instructional unit by way of grammatical structure, the unit now is framed by the context of a meaningful and practical application of language, namely, being able to both ask for and provide directions. The assessment likewise takes on a dramatically new form with this realization.

Textbooks in today's world language classrooms play a supportive role in creating a context for assessment and instruction. Texts produced since the release of the national standards include cultural thematic contexts, communicative activities, suggested adaptations for students with special learning needs, and performance tasks. Materials include reproducible blackline originals, workbooks, listening activities, CD-ROM practice activities, and access to online resources. Textbook company representatives agree that because today's textbooks provide packages with a wide variety of materials and activities, the teacher's role is to carefully select and sequence them to meet local learning objectives. Textbook producers typically encourage teachers to take charge of their instructional planning and remind them not to teach the textbook in a strict sequence from the first page to the last. Text materials provide a guide rather than a strict syllabus.

The teacher's role is to focus the curriculum, assessment, and then instruction by identifying the performance target. Creation of the unit involves identifying activities and experiences along a continuum to develop the desired language performance. Some activities provide exposure to the language element, others supply practice in manipulating the language to achieve increasingly more communicative purposes, and some give students the opportunity to apply the language element in a situation of real communication. The planning process also identifies the skills that are being developed, how these skills will be checked, the support or scaffolding of the language performances along the continuum, and at what point students will be responsible for an independent performance.

Setting Realistic Expectations for Performance

One very important aspect of this planning is keeping in mind realistic expectations for what students can do on their own in the target language. In the old paradigm of a linear sequence of vocabulary and grammar points, teachers expected students to master everything that was taught. Tests contained vocabulary taught earlier in the year and the grammar points from previous years. Although students do need to remember prior learning, the degree to which they will be able to use and apply such knowledge is a function of time. Consider a discrete grammar point such as object pronouns. Students may drill and practice object pronouns in isolation and learn to manipulate them in a particular unit. They do well on the very focused worksheets and test items that ask them to fill in blanks with the proper form. When thinking only about this one aspect of language, students perform fairly well. In the typical classroom, however, the teacher becomes frustrated later in the year when students do not use object pronouns properly in their paragraph writing. In reality, the teacher should expect such a drop in performance, because the students are only at the beginning round of internalizing the concept and are not yet at the stage at which they can independently apply it.

Learning a concept in isolation does not translate into independent use for life. The realistic expectation is that students will need repeated exposure, repeated practice in manipulation, and repeated reminders to check for a particular form in more open-ended writings. To set expectations for

students' performance in assessment, the teacher must consider what students will be able to do in the target language with or without help, in controlled or open-ended performances, and with the use of support devices or independently. This understanding of language acquisition will help the teacher realistically design appropriate language performances for each unit of instruction and criteria that will describe the type of performance that meets expectations.

World language curriculum design for K–12 must begin with the targeted language performances, realistically set for different learning stages, from beginners to advanced students. To help set such realistic expectations, educators will benefit from a study of the *ACTFL Performance Guidelines for K–12 Learners*, which, as previously noted, help educators identify the key characteristics of student performance along the pathway of developing language proficiency.

Designing Backward from the Assessment to Instruction

Clearly, this framework for making curriculum, assessment, and instructional decisions argues for the use of the backward design approach (Wiggins & McTighe, 1998). The assessment must be envisioned and designed before any instructional planning occurs. Further, the assessment for the unit needs to capture the knowledge and skills in their application, not in an abstract manner. To guide the design of unit-level assessment, balance across the three modes of communication is critical. Students should demonstrate their progress toward developing skill in interpersonal, conversational communication; interpretive listening or reading; and presentational writing or speaking. Gathering assessment evidence of these three modes (interpersonal, interpretive, and presentational) reminds the teacher and the students that all three are necessary to function and communicate in real-world situations. Students who feel they must plan their speaking before opening their mouth will be very hesitant to speak with native speakers in the spontaneous give-and-take of most social conversation. Those students who excel in negotiating conversations need to attend to the higher demands for accuracy of written communication, where misunderstanding is less easily resolved. Again, the message is clear: a balance of all three modes is essential.

The ACTFL led the development of a project to examine how to help classroom teachers evaluate students' language use, both in terms of the three modes of the communication standards and the K–12 performance guidelines. Three end-of-unit assessments form the core of this model of integrated performance assessment: an interpretive assessment task, an interpersonal communication task, and a presentational task. The assessment model was piloted in urban, suburban, and rural school districts in six states, coast to coast. Teachers reflecting on the effect of using this backward design model commented on the change in focus it gave to their teaching, specifically, that they kept the summative performance assessment tasks front and center as they made their daily lesson plans. They felt very confident about how clearly the end-of-unit assessments guided each and every instructional decision and how they could maximize the use of every minute in the classroom, knowing that each activity was leading directly to the final goal.

The teacher designing an integrated performance assessment for her instructional unit begins by realistically focusing on what she wants her students to do in the target language. From the K–12 performance guidelines, the teacher identifies the characteristics of language usage that form an appropriate target for the unit. Then, from within a meaningful context of rich content, the teacher decides exactly what the students will do to show their improvement in using the language in each of the three modes: interpretive, interpersonal, and presentational. These assessment targets then guide the development of all instruction, as the teacher sorts through the variety of materials, drills, practice activities, pair work, and resources that can support the development of the needed knowledge and skills within that context. Daily decisions are based on frequent monitoring of students' progress, gauging how close students are to demonstrating successful use of the language in each of the three modes.

Models of Performance Assessment for Languages

Integrated Performance Assessment (IPA): The IPA model is designed for individual teacher or school district use as a key component of curriculum design. This approach is reflected in some national assessment models as well. The original performance assessment model for languages is the Oral Proficiency Interview (OPI), developed in 1986 by the ACTFL, which then later developed the IPA. Interviewers go through rigorous training in order to administer and rate OPIs, making them valid and reliable assessments, but difficult for most classroom teachers to implement. Another challenge of the OPI is that for most K–12 programs, students move through only three benchmark levels: novice, intermediate, and advanced, and unless the elementary language instruction is continuous and regular, students will not make it to the advanced level. The limited increments of the OPI make it an instrument that will not satisfactorily chart student progress from year to year.

Other national assessment tools also have been influenced by the national standards' three modes of communication and the *ACTFL Performance Guidelines for K–12 Learners*. Designed for a variety of purposes, these tools are helpful in understanding the critical role that performance assessment plays in the design of curriculum and units of instruction.

National Assessment of Educational Progress (NAEP): The framework for the foreign language NAEP centered on an assessment of the three modes of communication. The test, which originally was scheduled for administration in 2004 (currently indefinitely postponed by the National Assessment Governing Board), included an assessment of interpretive reading, interpretive listening, presentational writing, and interpersonal conversation. The interpersonal task was administered through a phone call simulating a conversation between the student and a potential sister school. The rating scales were closely aligned with the K–12 performance guidelines' targets of novice, intermediate, and preadvanced (Kenyon, Farr, Mitchell, & Armengol, 2000).

The Minnesota Language Performance Assessment (MLPA): The MLPA includes tasks to evaluate students' proficiency in the areas of listening, reading, speaking, and writing. All assessments are given in a context that is sustained over a series of tasks; for example, to apply for an exchange program, students are asked to give basic information about themselves, to describe their family, to explain why they want to visit the target country, and, finally, to raise questions and issues they will want to discuss with the potential host family. These tasks gradually increase the complexity and depth of language that students use. This is intentional, in order to gather enough evidence for determining the student's proficiency level. The target is to determine whether the student is at the intermediate-low level on the ACTFL proficiency scale. Originally designed for placement and admission purposes at the University of Minnesota, the assessment has become a very useful tool for high school language teachers identifying performance targets for their own classroom (Center for Advanced Research on Language Acquisition, 2003).

Standards-Based Measurement of Proficiency (STAMP): STAMP provides online assessment of interpretive reading, speaking, and presentational writing. The assessment benchmarks its ratings to the novice-low through intermediate-mid levels on the ACTFL proficiency scale. Simulated conversational tasks are currently under development. STAMP is a very efficient tool for gathering student assessment data for the use of school districts or states (Language Learning Solutions, 2003).

Developing a Language Portfolio

These individual assessment tools provide a wide variety of useful data; however, no overall system for language assessment exists in the United States. For such a model, we turn to Europe, where the Council of Europe's education framework establishes the goal that all citizens will be trilingual. The Council of Europe asks all European Union countries to begin the study of a first nonnative language in elementary grades, adding a second nonnative language in secondary grades. To keep track of students' progress in learning languages and to capture the variety of ways they are acquiring proficiency, the Council of Europe has established *The European Language Portfolio* (Little & Perclová, 2002). In the portfolio, students keep track of all languages in which they have some proficiency. They identify how they have learned the language, for example, as a native language, as a language heard in their home or community, through academic study, through travel to another country, or by other means. Proficiency in each language is charted for listening, speaking, reading, and writing through a variety of descriptive statements. Students identify what they can do in each language in which they have some degree of proficiency. The message is that students develop different degrees of proficiency based on their need or motivation to learn and use a particular language.

Several states now are bringing the idea of language portfolios to their schools. Kentucky, Nebraska, and Indiana, among others, have begun to promote the use of a *LinguaFolio* to help students evaluate their progress toward learning languages (Moeller, Scow, & Van Houten, 2005). Their models ask students to look at a variety of language performances to showcase what they can do in the language. The *LinguaFolio* encourages students to examine classroom data, select best performances to showcase, and then keep track of the profile of what and how they have learned. The portfolio allows students to keep track not only of the language(s) they are learning in school but also to get "credit" for a wide variety of learning experiences, such as travel, immersion, Saturday schools, or community learning opportunities. Heritage speakers and users of a language can record what they realistically are able to do with the language, which may range from very informal, conversational language to the more formal, professional, or academic use of language.

Further, several school districts have developed common performance tasks for end-of-semester or end-of-course assessment of students' progress. School districts in Appleton, Wisc., and Davenport, Iowa, have designed language tasks that teachers administer at the end of each semester in the sequence of the language program, from middle school grades through senior high capstone courses. The assessments include interpretive, interpersonal, and presentational tasks, creating a profile of students' strengths and areas in need of attention. Teachers rate students' performances through rubrics that are based on the criteria of the K–12 performance guidelines, but are fine-tuned to show year-to-year progress. A powerful benefit is the resulting consensus among teachers on the language goals for courses. These assessments are ready to be reported in a district language portfolio, adding a summative measure of progress to the classroom samples of students' work.

Such language portfolios currently are designed to capture informal or classroom data on language performance, but lack a valid and reliable outside measure. Adding a national assessment instrument to the language profile will strengthen the way such a portfolio can be used beyond the individual

school. When students' skills can be compared to a national benchmark target, the portfolio also can be used for placement purposes across institutions, especially from high schools to postsecondary institutions. This verifying evidence will help teachers and students know with confidence whether they are on the right path toward developing higher levels of proficiency.

With these assessment systems in place, districts and states would be ready for world languages to join other disciplines as participants in the *Surveys of Enacted Curriculum (SEC)* (Council of Chief State School Officers [CCSSO], 2004). SEC, a project of CCSSO, currently involves mathematics, science, and English language arts. SEC provides a process for very closely examining the degree of alignment of state standards, assessment, and classroom instruction. State standards and the assessment instrument are coded to the discipline's specific content and the degree of cognitive demand. The scales and descriptive titles are designed specifically to fit the nature of each discipline. Following the coding of standards and assessments, classroom teachers complete a detailed survey in which they identify the amount of instructional time spent on each element of the discipline's content and the type of cognitive demand required of students. The result allows for either broad or very close examination of how well curriculum (as captured by the standards), assessment, and instruction are aligned. The data are a powerful tool for educators to examine their teaching practices.

With the development of a variety of performance assessment measures, policymakers and teachers of world languages are poised to engage in an examination of their curriculum, assessment, and instruction. National- or state-level assessments provide the measure for outside verification of classroom evidence. These assessments guide teachers' planning by providing the basis for backward design. The alignment with curriculum occurs when units are based on the same state and national standards as the assessments. The final alignment occurs when teachers examine how closely their classroom instruction leads to success on the assessments. Through this process, the real curriculum is revealed: what is taught, what is tested, and what is learned.

Ensuring Articulation

Assessments such as those described and supported in this chapter form a solid base of evidence for ensuring articulation. Lists of specific grammar concepts or vocabulary topics will vary even among teachers of the same course at the same school, and students will remember different amounts of each. Assuming that students will be ready to apply everything that was taught is foolhardy. Clearly, a broader view of what students have learned is needed. Such a realistic perspective comes through the development of performance targets to guide program and curriculum development. Such performance targets focus on what was learned, not merely what was taught, and, even more accurately, focus on what students can do with what was taught and learned. Envision how this framework could create different conversations between teachers at the elementary and middle school levels, between teachers at the middle school and senior high levels, and between those at the senior high and postsecondary levels. Instead of the accusatory tone adopted in reference to perceived poor instruction at the previous level—based on, for example, students not being able to conjugate verbs in a particular tense, not knowing the expected vocabulary, or not being able to produce specific *kanji* (Japanese characters)—teachers would base their discussion across institutional levels on actual evidence of what students can do.

This section has focused on designing curriculum via assessment targets. Figure 4 provides an example of a thematic unit on work and careers adapted for different proficiency levels by designing appropriate performance assessments for beginning students in elementary grades, intermediate students in middle school, and advanced students in senior high.

DESIGNING AND IMPLEMENTING FLEXIBLE WORLD LANGUAGE PROGRAMS

A standards-based and proficiency-oriented curriculum is best implemented through a program designed for flexibility. Because students do not move through an instructional sequence at the same speed or with the same motivation, decision makers should consider program options to meet a wider variety of student needs. Decisions affected by this new curriculum include how to accommodate students entering the program in different grades (K–12), how to effectively use technology in support of language learning, how to offer course options rather than a single course or level year after year, how to maintain language skills beyond formal course structures, how to place students who began their language learning in another school district, and how to create authentic environments in the language classroom. Program designers need to examine key decisions from the perspective of how best to develop higher levels of second-language proficiency in more students.

Considering the new emphasis on real-world applications for the language skills students are acquiring, designers of world language programs must ensure that form follows function. Program designers must reconsider their concepts of levels of instruction, credit based on seat time, and a single sequence of study. Program design must follow the newly configured curriculum, allowing students flexibility in moving through the language goals, with a variety of options available to them regarding content, course sequence, and learning mode. In the most common program model in place across the United States today, students do not demonstrate comparable achievement as they proceed lock-step through a course sequence based on nine months of a level-one course, followed by nine months of a

Figure 4
Thematic Unit Based on Performance Assessment Tasks

Clear performance assessment tasks for each of the three modes of communication (interpretive, interpersonal, and presentational)

Elementary Grades: Work and Careers (Introduction)—Who am I?/Who are you?

Interpretive: Watch a video of three students introducing themselves (videotaped when exchange students visited the school). Then, on a grid of topics that would logically be part of such an introduction, identify the topics actually mentioned and any details understood on each topic.	**Presentational:** Write a description of yourself accompanied by photos. The description will serve as a letter of introduction to a host family where you will be staying on a school trip abroad.	**Interpersonal:** To prepare for the first night at a host family's home, pair up and practice what you might say and what you might be asked by the host family. Introduce yourself by sharing the drawing prepared as part of the presentational assessment; ask questions about each other's likes and dislikes.

Middle School: Work and Careers (Future Plans)—How do I/you look at the world?

Interpretive: Read about a student your age from the target culture who describes her daily schedule, including interests, part-time jobs, school coursework, weekend activities, social life, and future plans. Summarize similarities and differences between the student's life and your own; draw some conclusions about how compatible you would be with this student, giving reasons for your conclusions.	**Presentational:** Give a presentation about your life and interests. Indicate how these activities reflect your personality. Include some possibilities for your future in terms of career, study, travel, and pursuing personal interests.	**Interpersonal:** Discuss with a group of classmates your plans for high school. Indicate what kinds of courses you will take and how they will prepare you for your future plans. Discuss career options and which ones interest or don't interest you and why.

Senior High: Work and Careers (Preparing to Work)—What do I/you think and feel?

Interpretive: Listen to a presentation by a guest speaker concerning how he uses languages on the job. Discuss how important knowledge of another language and cross-cultural understanding are to success in this career. Include any questions that the speaker may not have directly answered, hypothesizing why he may have avoided a direct answer.	**Interpersonal:** Discuss in a group of four to five people your options for career choices based on a variety of criteria, including: availability of jobs, competition for jobs, salary, security, opportunity for travel, opportunity to use another language, opportunity for advancement, personal satisfaction, service to humanity, and so on. Discuss the pros and cons of each career possibility.	**Presentational:** Write a letter applying for an internship in a foreign company where you would like to work. State your qualifications, your career goals, and your knowledge of languages and cross-cultural understanding—anything that you feel could enhance your candidacy.

Source: Adapted from *Planning Curriculum for Learning World Languages* (pp. 78, 90, 106), by P. Sandrock, 2002, Madison, WI: Wisconsin Department of Public Instruction. Copyright 2002 by the Wisconsin Department of Public Instruction. Adapted with permission.

level-two course, and continuing on until they exhaust the courses offered. Even though their achievement may vary greatly, all students move on to the next level the following term whether their grade is an *A* or a *D*. But in order to learn to use a new language, students need to have multiple paths to progress through a program. Options and flexibility are key criteria for creating a language-learning program that will truly deliver the goals of the standards. So, what program options can deliver the quality instruction that will build second-language proficiency in more students?

Proficiency Versus Seat Time

The first hurdle to overcome in program design is the concept of a language course equaling 180 days of attendance. Teachers would agree that even students starting in a beginning language course bring different background experiences to the class. Some students may know a few words in the target language; some may have had a short course or experience outside of school exposing them to some words or phrases in the language; some may have visited a country where the language is spoken; and some may have relatives who speak the language. Students show differences in their knowledge of and skill in using the target language right from the beginning of a level-one course. As students move through the course sequence, level by level, these differences only increase. At least in a level-one course, the teacher knows exactly the common knowledge, skills, and activities students have experienced in the language-learning classroom. At any subsequent level, the teacher cannot assume a common background experience among the students. By the time students reach the fourth or fifth year of a language sequence, they exhibit quite a range of ability to use the language: some students will show strengths in writing, others will display expertise in negotiating conversation, some will demonstrate a facility for understanding written pas-

sages, and still others will excel at interpreting spoken language. As the course content, both instruction and assessment, must be adapted to this wide range of student performance, so must course options vary to meet the application needs and interests of all students. The language learner no longer fits a single profile for learning and, as such, courses and sequences need to reflect variety.

How can this happen when enrollment in a particular language may be limited, a school has only one language teacher who cannot take on numerous independent study students, or courses at different levels are combined into a single teaching hour?

Combined Multiyear Courses

Upper-level courses often need to be combined due to enrollment numbers. In moderate-sized and smaller high schools, for example, student enrollment may not meet the number needed to create a separate section of a course, and in this era of tight budgets, the number of students that need to be enrolled in a course before it is actually offered is rising. Where language teachers could count on class sizes of 20–25 students in the 1980s and early 1990s, they now are reporting that class size minimums of 30 are increasingly common. This rising cut-off number for offering a language level is especially challenging in small schools, where frequently only one section of an upper-level course is scheduled and may simply be dropped when not enough students sign up.

Given this situation, administrative and teaching staffs need to develop creative solutions, rather than simply dropping the next language learning opportunity for students. When faced with a combination of third- and fourth-year students in a single class hour, or fourth- and fifth-year students, teachers need to rethink their curriculum content. Trying to run two separate content courses within a single hour merely frustrates the teacher and short-changes the students, who end up receiving only half of their expected instructional time as the teacher alternates teaching between the two levels.

A stronger approach is to design a two-year sequence of content in which themes are selected on the basis of their interest for the age range of students in the combined course (e.g., sophomores through seniors), as well as the adaptability of the theme to students of differing language profiles. Consider, for example, how the thematic unit of current social and political issues in countries that speak the target language could be used to teach both third- and fourth-year students in the same class hour. Envision students forming groups based on specific issues they want to explore. To gain background knowledge, students could work together to access Internet sources. Differences in language proficiency are not critical to this activity, because students use skim and scan techniques to browse for pertinent resources (such as articles, graphs and charts, or interviews). Students work together to summarize the information they find, each contributing within their proficiency level, with some students writing lists, others jotting down key phrases, and some able to generate brief paragraphs. Small-group discussion could also occur across "levels" of language proficiency as students work to understand and be understood, sharing the information they find and creating bullet-point summaries.

To challenge students to use language at or slightly above their comfort levels, the teacher would then create differentiated tasks to build on this common base of knowledge. On a given issue, third-year students might compare and contrast two points of view within the target culture or compare the predominant view within the target culture to that held in the United States. Their language performance would show more concrete use of language, quoting examples found, following learned patterns of language, and perhaps using lists and phrases to set up the contrasts. Fourth-year students might be challenged to create a debate in which they have to think more spontaneously. They could also write an editorial stating their opinion on the issue. This is just one example of how students at different levels can participate together in the same unit of instruction.

At Monroe High School in Wisconsin, students may enroll in a course called Spanish in Context. Students begin the course as second-year students of Spanish, but they may stay in the course for their third year of language study as well. This is a regularly scheduled course that provides flexibility for students. The teacher has a two-year curriculum of units targeted to help students improve their language skills in order to transition from the beginning language course to a more advanced course. Some students take the course for one year; others take the course for two years. What is constant is the language proficiency target; what varies is the amount of time it may take students to achieve that goal. This is quite the opposite of most high school courses, where the time frame to earn a credit remains constant in the form of semester or year-long segments, but all students do not reach the achievement target equally, as reflected in the range of grades they receive.

Movement Based on Proficiency

Another solution is to build in flexibility for how students move through a course sequence. Menasha (Wisc.) Joint School District has changed its high school course titles and students' movement through the language courses on the basis of the experience of the first students to begin learning languages in kindergarten. In each elementary school, one world language is taught to all the students in that school (two schools teach Japanese, two teach Spanish, and one teaches German). The amount of time per week for language instruction increases from 40 minutes per week in kindergarten to 150 minutes per week in 5th grade. The curriculum was developed for each new grade level based on the real performance achieved by students in the previous grade level. In other words, the 5th grade world language curriculum was not developed until language teachers had a clear sense of what the students were able to do in the 4th grade.

When the students reached the end of 8th grade, the district had to decide where to place them in the existing, fairly traditional senior high sequence of first- through fifth-year language courses. Staff decided to base this decision, again, on the real performance of students. Teachers designed prompts to elicit both written and spoken samples of students' use of the target language. These performance assessments were administered to students in 8th grade, as well as to students at the end of the first- and second-year high school language courses. Teachers then sorted the language samples into piles of "good," "average," and "poor," without knowing the grade levels of the students. When the grade levels were added to the language samples, the teachers were not surprised to find that the 8th grade students had performed as well as, if not better than, the students in their second year of high school language instruction. As an initial decision, given that their language performance most closely matched that of students at the end of the high school second-year course, all 8th grade students were placed for 9th grade in the third-year language course. This worked well, but the staff decided to explore even further the idea of proficiency-based placement.

Realizing that the same approach of using language performance for placement purposes could be applied to all high school language courses, the language department looked at how to provide options for all students to move through their sequence of courses. They designed, and the administration approved, a plan for continuous monitoring of student performance for the purpose of moving students to the next level of instruction when their language profile matched that of the next course. Courses are now named Beginning, Transitional, Intermediate, and Advanced. Students may stay in a course for one, two, three, or four semesters. The criterion for moving to the next course is not seat time but language performance. Each semester, a student has the opportunity to move to the next course, if the student's language profile looks like that of students in that next course. The transcript reflects seat time, with each course semester labeled as A, B, C, or D, but the true achievement of the student is marked by progress through the course titles (Beginning through Advanced). The act of changing the deciding factor for movement through the course sequence from seat time to true language proficiency offers a workable, practical solution to the need for proficiency-based placement.

Moving Beyond a Single Linear Sequence

Taking the idea of student options one step further, program designers need to ask themselves whether a single sequence of courses is the only workable program model. In other subject areas, a general common core of knowledge and skill might be considered the beginning point. At some point, however, students may select from among multiple options within those disciplines to extend their learning. English language arts programs, for example, often provide a common set of courses for freshmen and sophomores in high schools before opening up the course sequence to a variety of options designed to appeal to students' specific interests and needs. After a general 9th grade English course, for instance, many high school sophomores take one semester of composition and one semester of speech. This two-year basic core of work in English language arts provides students with the skills, knowledge, and experiences that enable them to move to the next level of challenge, but not necessarily in a controlled sequence. Juniors and seniors often are able to choose from a wide variety of semester-length courses targeting their interests and needs, selecting from courses such as creative writing, American literature, journalism, debate, drama, and more. Students in their fourth year of English don't stop increasing their skills in using English while working with third-year students; rather, they are challenged to improve from their current skill level while participating in common research, discussion, and group work. Similarly, in social studies, after completing a general course sequence (commonly comprising general world history and U.S. history) in which students develop basic skills, a wide range of options is made available in the areas of history, economics, psychology, and other social sciences. The sequence is not controlled, other than to label courses as introductory or advanced.

What would such an approach look like in world languages? Program designers would identify the basic skills and knowledge that would enable students to be more independent in their study of and more confident in their use of the target language. A description of such basic proficiency might include the ability to tell a simple story, knowledge of narrating in different time frames (present and past), and language skills sufficient to meet basic survival and social needs. Such a basic set of skills could be targeted for approximately two years of senior high instruction. At that point, courses could be offered with the designation of intermediate or advanced. Students, based on their language performance profile, could enroll in any of the courses designated within their learning target (intermediate or advanced). An individual student's route through the courses would not matter; rather, the emphasis would be on improvement through coursework and experiences of interest to the student. Course offerings could focus on content descriptions, rather than on grammatical concepts. Rather than a single yearlong option of fourth-year lan-

guage after third-year language, students might choose from among semester-length courses such as "Exploring the Target Culture Through Its Arts," "Understanding Contemporary Issues in the Target Country," "Research and Careers in the Target Language," "Literature," or "Uncovering Cultural Attitudes Through Media."

Language Maintenance Strategies

One more program option to consider is how best to serve students who want to maintain their language skills when schedule conflicts or other course requirements preclude their enrollment in a regularly scheduled language course. Other than classes that meet for 90 or 180 days, how can a school offer options that provide sufficient rigor and accountability to ensure that students will maintain or improve their language skills? Some schools already have explored such possibilities. Standards-based curriculum, assessment, and instruction need not be limited to existing course structures. Language learning targets could be set, assessments designed, and instructional coaching facilitated to enable students to enroll in a variety of language maintenance "courses." Such learning experiences would allow students to continue to work on their second-language skills, even when they are not able to enroll in a regularly scheduled course.

What would such options look like? Students might provide assistance to other language learners by serving as language lab or computer lab assistants. The language-maintenance student would commit to a certain number of hours of lab assistance, consisting of tutoring other language students, searching for authentic materials, or editing students' short compositions or essays. The language teacher would oversee the student's work and assign projects for him to work on (when not helping other students) that would provide practice in using the target language.

Another example would be to provide language "opportunities." Students could sign up as regular participants in one particular type of event or participate in a variety of events, with a certain number required to receive .25, .5, or 1 course credit. Imagine language tables in the school cafeteria at which only the target language can be spoken for the entire lunch period (for example, a French table on Mondays, a Japanese table on Wednesdays, and a Spanish table on Fridays). Or consider the results if one teacher per language were assigned to serve as a language coach for a semester as part of her supervision duty. Flexibility could be afforded regarding the weekly schedule for the supervision hour. For example, the teacher might schedule it twice during a free period, once during a lunch hour, and twice after school. This language coach would work with students in a variety of ways to help them use the target language for research, interviews, or information gathering for projects in other classes or disciplines. Students might need to do research using the target language for courses in other subject areas. Examples: examining French sources for information about the attitude of the French toward the United States before, during, and after World War II and preparing a report on the findings for a social studies course; exploring the market for a product to be exported to South America for a business course; and looking for songs from countries where the target language is spoken that have a theme similar to a poem or popular American song. In addition, students might need help with vocabulary and teaching ideas in order to tutor English language learners whose native language is the language they are studying. For instance, a student might come to the language coach for ideas on how best to help Spanish-speaking students with their math homework.

The language teacher does not need to know the content of each of these subject areas in order to help each student; rather, her role is to oversee students' application of their target language skills and to mark progress in how well students improve those skills. The language teacher would use the supervision hour to help students use authentic materials, assist in searching for resources in the target language, evaluate how well students use interpretive skills, and provide feedback for their written or oral presentation of information.

Another approach is to help heritage-language students improve their use of the heritage language. Heritage-language students exhibit a wide range of proficiency, depending on the type and level of immersion in the language they have had. If such a student grew up in the United States, for example, she may have virtually no literacy training in her heritage language. She may have only speaking and listening skills and only at an informal, social level. This student would need experiences in reading and writing her heritage language and in adjusting it to fit formal and informal situations. Language teachers could provide heritage students with experiences such as creating questions and then formally interviewing a native speaker, summarizing research, writing up reports, and giving presentations. These assignments might occur outside of a regular course through regularly scheduled coaching sessions.

Participating in these language "opportunities" could add up to actual credit. Credit could be awarded through a combination of the number of events, activities, or sessions that a student completes, with an evaluation of the student's use of the target language to show the degree of improvement made. Giving credit for these language maintenance strategies encourages students to become lifelong learners and practitioners of languages. It also gives value to such activities, not only to the student earning the credit but also in the eyes of the entire school and community.

Multiple Entry Points

The key to offering multiple entry points into a language program is to avoid duplication and starting over. The National Council of State Supervisors of Foreign Languages argues that the guiding principle for program design is to build on the language proficiency developed in the previous grade level:

Curriculum Connects from One Course to the Next: Effective middle school world language programs develop proficiency in a language in addition to English. Therefore, curriculum at the middle school level must impact the curriculum at the high school [level]. Initial experiences in a world language begin the movement from zero proficiency toward near-native-level proficiency in the language. Each succeeding contact increases a student's level of proficiency. If initial experiences occur in the elementary grades, students should not repeat the same experience in middle school, but should have the opportunity to continue with more specific study of a chosen language. The middle school world language program must build on the skills developed in any existing elementary language experiences in the district.

Likewise, if sampling of languages occurs in one grade level of the middle school, students should be able to continue study of a chosen language in each succeeding grade level in the middle school. The middle school world language program should articulate with programs at the senior high level. Students who develop a beginning level of proficiency in using the language through middle school instruction should not have to start back at a beginning level in senior high. This would not be tolerated in any other subject area, such as math,

science, music, or technical education, and it must be avoided in language learning as well.

The language curriculum must "ripple up" from one course to the next, based on what students can do with the language (not based on the exact vocabulary or grammatical structures covered). This will ensure that each level of instruction builds upon the preceding one. In other words, students will be able to function at ever-more sophisticated levels as they move through the language sequence. (Webb & Sandrock, 2003, pp. 5–6)

In order to ensure that students are advanced appropriately—that is, as a result of demonstrated proficiency rather than a listing of grammatical structures and vocabulary topics covered in the previous level's course(s)—all components that reflect students' proficiency level need to be in sync: curriculum, course sequences and options, assessments, and portfolios. If any of these components are based solely on students' knowledge of discrete grammar points or lists of vocabulary, then students will have no flexibility in starting at different points or moving at different speeds. Not only must the curriculum support proficiency-oriented learning, but course options must also consider students' proficiency levels, and assessments must make students' proficiency levels transparent to each teacher, parent, and student.

Of course, providing a variety of points of entry into the language-learning program is not simply a matter of cutting and pasting the senior high curriculum into an equal number of hours of instruction for students in elementary grades or middle school. Students at different ages and grades learn differently. Therefore, the world language program must be designed to provide specific skills in using the language, rather than simply teaching about the language or its culture in English. Only with an emphasis on language use can a program truly prove its value in starting before senior high school.

Guiding Principles for Program Design

A guiding principle for program design is to offer longer sequences in languages, rather than trying to expose students to all possible languages before allowing them to begin to progress toward a functional level of proficiency in any single language. Let students begin as soon as possible to develop proficiency in one language. Then, once students reach a level of language proficiency that is easily sustained, they will benefit from learning a third language. If students spend too much time sampling one language after another, the program expends its resources and students wind up having no functional ability in any language. Programs do not last when they are unable to provide proof that students learn anything worthwhile or lasting.

Elementary Grades (K–5): A successful guiding principle at this level is to teach one language in a building. This creates a link between the staff and the target culture as the entire school community starts to view itself as "the Japanese school" or "the French school." The school is more likely to build a sister school relationship with a school abroad, to take advantage of artists-in-residence programs linked to the target culture, and to seek other ways to model the target culture in the school. Classroom teachers can use phrases in the target language for classroom management purposes or to move students into groups. In addition, the "permission" language in the school can employ the target language (e.g., May I go to the bathroom? May I get a drink of water? May I borrow a pencil?). If students will have the opportunity to learn other languages in middle school, a successful strategy has been to assign each elementary school one of those languages, thus equally distributing the languages so that each receives some continuing students in the

middle school. For example, if the middle school offers German, Arabic, and Spanish, then one language could be taught at each of the three elementary schools feeding into that middle school. Thus, the 6th grade students would have the following options upon entering middle school: continue studying the language they were learning in elementary school, become a beginner in a new language, or both.

Elementary schools teaching languages need to plan for how they will deal with students entering in later grades. For example, when the language instruction begins in 1st grade, what will the new 4th grade student do? A highly successful strategy is to keep the new 4th grader in with the other 4th grade students during language instruction, but to provide support through an assigned "study buddy" (who can explain to the new student the one word, expression, or concept that will unlock the mystery of what is going on in class), once-weekly catch-up sessions (perhaps provided by a fellow student), and assessment rubrics tailored to the student's performance level.

Middle School (Grades 6–8): If students have had language-learning opportunities in the elementary grades, then they should have three options in middle school: continue the language begun in the elementary grades, add another language, or substitute another language. When language learning has begun at the elementary level, little rationale exists for requiring an exploratory course at the middle school level to sample a variety of languages. The incoming students already know how to learn a language. If other languages are available in the middle school, the students' intrinsic motivation, personal goals, and even curiosity will lead them to select a language to study. Forcing experiences in three or four languages rarely dramatically changes the enrollment patterns of students. Meaningful curriculum units team-taught with an English language arts or social studies teacher might prove a more successful way to expose students to new languages they might otherwise be leery of taking. A highly successful model based on just such a strategy was developed at Cherokee Middle School in Madison, Wisc., and involved a Chinese teacher working with the two-hour, team-taught English language arts and social studies class. The three teachers created a unit exploring the language, culture, and history of China. Students overcame their fear of understanding such a "foreign" language, took pride in writing Chinese characters and being able to read them, and gained deeper perspectives on Chinese people and culture. This was a language experience brought to the existing curriculum: it took advantage of an appropriate forum for sampling a new language and no additional time was carved out to offer the experience. The English language arts and social studies teachers saw their curriculum and learning goals seamlessly blended with those of the Chinese teacher.

Senior High (Grades 9–12): Similar to their options in middle school, students with prior experiences learning a language should be able to continue the study of that language, add other languages, or switch to another language altogether. Only with long sequences of study will students build up sufficient language proficiency to ensure that they will not lose their abilities when they stop official coursework in that language and take up a new (third) language. Numerous ideas have already been offered for creating flexibility in learning, both for progress through the courses and for new course offerings. As at the other levels of study, flexibility based on students' language proficiency is the key to providing multiple entry points at the senior high level.

Creating Authentic Classroom Environments

An obvious first step toward creating authentic classroom environments is to employ authentic materials—that is, materials designed for native speakers in the target culture. Bringing such materials into the classroom helps students become comfortable with being immersed in the new language. Language teachers need to approach the use of such materials by teaching comprehension strategies rather than teaching all the possible unknown vocabulary prior to looking at the material. Consider how native speakers approach such authentic materials: they also may not know every word used, yet they do not let a lack of vocabulary end their attempt to understand the material. Teachers need to teach students the skills to access materials as a native speaker would, not by knowing every word but by skimming and scanning; hypothesizing on the basis of format clues, illustrations, captions, and key words; and looking for details that either reinforce or change the original hypothesis, thereby bringing the students ever closer to the full meaning.

A second strategy for achieving authenticity is the use of technology. Textbooks used to become outdated almost the day they were printed. Many German teachers, for example, had to use textbooks that described the Berlin Wall for seven years after it had been removed! Today, textbook companies provide Web sites that are regularly updated, adding new readings and activities for teachers to bring into the classroom. Beyond the textbook, teachers can download headlines directly from newspapers around the world. Students can identify the key local, national, and international stories from a newspaper abroad and compare the list to their local news source. Along these same lines, students can see how long a particular story maintains prominent coverage and whether the coverage lasts longer locally or abroad. Through technology, students can learn not just information about popular culture such as songs, movies, and TV, but can also explore how cultural perspectives compare or contrast on any given topic. Further, it is worth noting that the Internet is not an

English-only vehicle; the current estimate is that 67.2 percent of Web users are not native speakers of English (Internet World Stats, 2005).

Technology also provides connections to real users of the language. A variety of Web sites exist to connect language teachers interested in setting up official or unofficial sister school relationships. To get beyond mere pen pal exchanges describing family, home, pets, likes, and dislikes, the focus of the exchange needs to be a substantive project. Consider an environmental survey: students explore what issues are the same or different in their community and their sister school's; examine how each community or culture looks at the particular environmental issue; and find out what solutions are being tried or implemented in each community. Another route to developing deeper understanding across cultures is through poetry exchanges: students write poems and send them to the sister school with accompanying photos. This immediately leads to a deeper exchange of questions and comments, which reveal cultural perspectives far better than a simple "What do you like to do after school?" exchange could. Schools have arranged successful exchanges of students' art projects in order to bring the sister classroom to the attention of the entire school, thereby raising the cultural awareness of the entire school population, including parents. Some schools get the entire community involved in the exchange by soliciting sponsors for the transportation of projects, hosts for visitors from the sister school's community, and attendance at open house events. One school with a Japanese sister school arranged the costly shipping of *taiko* drums given by the sister school by soliciting donations from local companies. The cultural festival that used the drums was attended by many community members, because they felt that they, too, had a connection to the sister school.

Connections, comparisons, and communities are three of the national standards' goal areas for learning languages, goals that teachers are often at a loss to know how to implement. The preceding examples of how to create an authentic environment in the language classroom provide glimpses into the variety of ways to connect to other disciplines, develop a deeper level of cultural comparison, and show students how to participate in multilingual communities at home and abroad. Creating authentic situations for real communication through the target language not only engages students but also shows them that the language has a deeper value and application far beyond the original classroom tasks.

Living Through Technology

The decision of how and when to use technology or alternate means of learning must be made on the basis of how well students will achieve the learning targets. Technology is only a means; the development of language proficiency is the end. Another significant variable for evaluating the use of technology in support of language learning is the age or grade level of the students.

Numerous variations on distance learning exist. The key points of difference are: synchronous (the teacher delivers instruction at the same time that the students are receiving it) versus asynchronous (instruction is delivered via prerecorded segments); stand-alone (provides all of the necessary instruction, practice, and assessment) versus supplemental (brings auxiliary components to the learning, such as authentic materials or a variety of native speakers); and teacher-evaluated (students turn in assignments and tests to a central instructor for grading and feedback) versus self-evaluated (students or a local facilitator grade tests and assignments).

Some distance-learning providers place limits on the number of students who can be in the course at each site, often due to the type of supervision available. A media center director supervising students by watching them through the windows of a distance learning classroom would want only a few students in a class, whereas an onsite facilitator learning a language along with the students would probably be comfortable with more students in a class.

Research in both high school and elementary programs emphasizes the critical role of the on-site facilitator. Kubota (1999) identified the interest of the on-site facilitator as a highly significant variable linked to student learning in a distance-learning classroom. When the facilitator engages in the learning, students are more motivated to actively participate, and they identify the facilitator as someone of whom they can ask questions or seek assistance. The facilitator learning with the students simultaneously models learning and monitors student work.

An example of effective distance learning at the elementary level and a testament to the importance of the on-site facilitator is the IN-VISION Project, a collaboration of schools in Iowa and Nebraska organized through the Nebraska Department of Education. The project evaluation underscored the key role played by the bilingual aide serving as on-site facilitator. The instruction came via a video program for learning Spanish, geared toward students in the elementary grades. The distance-learning technology not only brought instruction twice a week, but was also used for training the bilingual aides. Each week, they received instruction as to what to do before, during, and after each video lesson. These aides already knew the language and culture; the training gave them the teaching skills they needed to prepare students for an upcoming video or the lesson follow-up activities, where students could apply what they had learned. The study underscored the importance of a trained and competent language specialist to interact with students. A study on the effectiveness of video programs for teaching languages to young children underscored this role of videos as supple-

mental to students' face-to-face interactions with a trained and competent language specialist (Rhodes & Pufahl, 2004).

In order to maximize the effect of the local language teacher, smaller districts might consider how to use distance learning for upper-level courses. As in other subject areas, the number of students enrolled at the beginning of the study of the discipline decreases as students move into advanced courses. The number of students taking physics classes, for example, is far smaller than the number in 8th grade science. In addition, students who have continued in a subject area beyond the basic levels and beyond a required level of instruction are generally highly interested in the topic and would benefit most from the independence and trust inherent in distance learning. Rather than using distance learning for middle school courses or beginning language sections, districts might consider having the local language educator teach the language courses directly in grades 6–10 and offer distance learning for students who want to continue their study of the language in grades 11 and 12. These students are motivated, show independence as learners, and generally are fewer in number, making supervision less of an issue for the distance-learning arrangements.

Online learning is another option for using technology in language courses. The main difference between online and distance learning is the asynchronous nature of online learning. Generally, online learning is packaged as a complete course, but the assignments may be self-checked or evaluated by a human instructor. Instruction delivered solely online lacks the interpersonal communication component, a critical element of language learning. Students can learn, practice, and perform interpretive and presentational tasks, but spontaneous conversations are not usually part of such courses. For this reason, planners should give attention to creative ways to develop conversational ability to supplement the online learning.

Technology also provides great opportunities for student assessment. In the past, teachers avoided assessment of interpersonal conversations because of the time involved in recording each pair of students. The teacher would try to monitor two students (while also monitoring the classroom), who would go into the hallway, sit at two desks, turn on an audiotape recorder, have their conversation, and then, if they remembered, turn off the recorder. By contrast, today's computer labs make it possible for the teacher to take students into the lab, randomly pair up students, have all students talk about the given topic for 2–5 minutes, and then walk away with a CD-ROM recording of all the paired conversations. Finding and returning to any given pair's conversation is thus made easy. When logistics do not present a problem, teachers are more likely to plan assessment of conversation. This provides important feedback to students and reinforces the balance of the three modes of communication. In addition, the class grade is not based solely on written work because assessment evidence gives value to conversational skills.

Program Design Summation

Good program design guarantees a structure that assists students as they move from a point of no or limited facility in the target language to increasing comfort and confidence in using the language as a native speaker would. The guiding principles for implementing such programs must include

- Flexibility in how students move through the system.

- Advancement based on proficiency rather than on days spent in class.

- Courses identified by proficiency levels.

- Course options to meet the interests of a wider variety of students.

- Attention to the unique needs of heritage speakers.

- Options to help students maintain language skills beyond course structures.

- Opportunities to learn, practice, and apply language skills in authentic settings.

- Innovative use of technology to support language learning.

THE ROLE OF SUPERVISORS AND CURRICULUM COORDINATORS

The role of supervisors and curriculum coordinators must necessarily change in order to develop this new model of curriculum, assessment, and instruction. A key task for these leaders is to support professional development for the front-line implementers, and this is accomplished best through collaboration and support, rather than tightly controlled supervision. Teachers need a forum for learning, experimenting with, and sharing classroom best practices for language learning. Supervisors and curriculum coordinators, then, become the agents of change to focus world language programs on the development of students' proficiency in using the target language.

What is the role of the world language supervisor or curriculum coordinator in implementing successful communicative-based world language programs? To answer this question, one must first examine the characteristics of effective programs. World language programs that achieve the vision of the standards manifest, to some degree, all of the following (Gilzow & Branaman, 2000):

- Curriculum based on both state and national standards (communicative-based, organized around themes incorporating real-life situations, assessed by a variety of strategies).

- Periodic program evaluation.

- Articulation from the elementary to middle school level and from middle school to high school level.

- Ongoing professional development that is directly focused on student achievement and learning needs.

- Inclusion of students with diverse needs.

- Evidence of well-informed K–12 administrators who have been provided with information on what constitutes effective second-language learning and how it benefits students throughout the education continuum.

- Support from parents, teachers, board members, and other members of the community.

- Effective supervisory leadership.

In reviewing these characteristics, it is apparent that the world language supervisor has a key role to play in making each of these factors a reality in the district program. Effective world language supervisors possess a knowledge base in second-language acquisition theory, current instructional methodology and assessment strategies, and the latest research and best practices, both in the field and in the broader educational context. In addition, these individuals typically bring other leadership qualities to the table. First and foremost, they are passionate and relentless in what they do. For world language supervisors, this is critically important, given that they must convince the educational community that achieving competence in a second language takes a long time and happens best in well-articulated programs with appropriate time allocations and effective instructional practices. They also are able to clearly articulate how the goals of second-language learning support learning in other areas of the curriculum, as well as achievement of current national and state literacy goals. These individuals more often than not are visible

within the entire school community; are viewed as innovators and collaborators with other curriculum areas; and are active members of local, state, and national organizations devoted to learning and teaching.

According to the National Association of District Supervisors of Foreign Languages (NADSFL, n.d.), in order to provide a high-quality program that implements the national standards and serves the needs of students, local school districts must have content specialists with subject-specific expertise to facilitate needed change. School districts that depend on generalists to supervise their language programs miss out on the knowledge and ability that world language specialists offer. It is impossible for any one individual to possess the depth of knowledge in every subject area that is necessary for an effective instructional program, therefore, it behooves each district to have a world language specialist who is knowledgeable about current research and best practice in the field and disseminates that knowledge to others.

Figure 5 defines five areas of responsibility for the world language supervisor, as identified by NADSFL: what is taught, how it is taught, what it is taught with, how it is enriched, and how it is explained to others.

According to Michael Fullan (2002), well-known author on change research, "sustainability depends on many leaders—thus, the qualities of leadership must be attainable by many, not just a few" (p. 20). How, then, does the profession build capacity at the supervisory level to cultivate the necessary leadership to implement and sustain reform-based second-language programs? A strategy that has been successful in New Jersey is the formation of a Supervisors of World Languages Regional Roundtables initiative. The roundtables serve as a professional forum for district supervisors of world languages and other administrators responsible for

---

Figure 5
Areas of Responsibility for a World Language Supervisor

What Is Taught: Curriculum Design and Implementation
The supervisor of world languages provides leadership in designing and implementing a world language program (curriculum, assessment, and instruction) that develops real language proficiency in all students, including those with differing learning styles, abilities, and interests.

How It Is Taught: Staff Recruitment and Development
The supervisor of world languages provides professional development and assistance to individual teachers based on current research, trends in world language teaching, and district needs.

What It Is Taught With: Teaching Materials and Equipment
The supervisor of world languages analyzes needs; researches options; and oversees selection of instructional materials, including textbooks, technology, and other resources.

How It Is Enriched: Districtwide Activities
The supervisor of world languages provides leadership in developing and carrying out districtwide world language curricular and extracurricular activities for students.

How It Is Explained to Others: Information and Advocacy
The supervisor of world languages—in the role of liaison among language teachers, administrators, and the community—serves as a resource on effective practices, articulates the language program goals, and provides updates on requirements and legislation.

---

the implementation of world language programs. The goals of the initiative are to

■ Assist supervisors with the ongoing design, assessment, and implementation of world language programs;

■ Provide professional development for instructional improvement based on cognitive research, second-language acquisition theories, current practices in second language teaching, and district needs;

■ Promote advocacy for the study of world languages;

■ Work collaboratively with colleagues in other content areas and professional organizations to facilitate standards-based reform in New Jersey schools; and

■ Recognize and cultivate supervisory leadership throughout the state. (Jensen, 2002)

Regional roundtable meetings are held in the northern, central, and southern areas of the state four times a year and are hosted by school districts in each respective region. At these meetings, supervisors are given the opportunity to talk about common problems, discuss problem-solving strategies, and share success stories. The meetings are primarily devoted to collaborative work on one or several of the projects selected by the group as priorities during the academic year, such as revising curricula based on the backward design model (Wiggins & McTighe, 1998) or developing a high school curriculum template for use by supervisors and staff.

The regional roundtables were responsible for creating and implementing a statewide initiative of K–12 model programs and an award process to acknowledge district supervisory leadership. Further, they have had an effect on the development of state documents and policy by providing feedback to the New Jersey Department of Education during the revision of the world language content standards and establishment of a statewide proficiency level to meet the high school graduation requirement.

The first and last meetings of each school year are statewide, involve supervisors from all regions, and focus on a relevant topic of concern in world language education addressed by a recognized authority on the subject. In addition to these meetings, professional development workshops, designed specifically for supervisors, are offered at intervals during the course of the year. For example, supervisors have been offered sessions on how to train their staffs in the use of performance-based assessment. These sessions included materials to be used as training tools, suggestions on conducting training sessions, participation in troubleshooting discussions related to training, the sharing of training results, and planning for continued training and evaluation of the process.

The supervisors' roundtables can be likened to a professional community of learners who have discovered the power of discussing practice together. Roundtable activities have allowed supervisors to learn about and learn through different perspectives and experience the value of giving and receiving meaningful feedback. They also have enabled supervisors to meet at regular intervals to build knowledge, examine each other's work, and keep abreast of the latest research. Most importantly, the roundtables have empowered supervisors to take on a new role by actively participating in creating structures to facilitate change both at the district and state levels.

Another critical component for capacity building is providing ongoing support for language teachers. An example is the creation of networks to sustain professional development throughout the year. A trained cadre of presenters might offer a local, informal workshop for language teachers to facilitate the sharing of teaching strategies. Similarly, a state organization could develop a regional net-

work of study groups facilitated by trained leaders, with expert-provided study guides to assist the facilitator. Also, regional mentors could provide coaching in the teaching of languages to new teachers in their areas. Such networks could meet in person or virtually through videoconferencing, e-mail list servers, or an online support site. All of the above measures address the need to retain qualified staff.

The redefined role of the world language supervisor in this era of educational reform is to promote collaboration and change, rather than maintaining the control, order, and efficiency of the current system (i.e., writing observation reports, scheduling, and ordering materials). A professional learning community, such as the supervisors' roundtables, provides educators with the opportunity to influence or change set practices within and across their respective areas of specialization. (For an example of one supervisor's role in bringing about curricular change in world language instruction, visit this chapter of the *Curriculum Handbook* online at www.ascd.org/handbook.)

According to Rick Donato, teacher educator and researcher at the University of Pittsburgh, "Leadership emanate[s] from collaborations to understand one's local situation, the various perspectives on critical issues, and the possible futures of fundamental change that potentially improve the lives of teachers, learners, and the profession" (2000, p. 116). Implementing the vision of the standards requires that supervisory leadership move beyond technical management, organization, and information transmission. Leaders for change become learners in real reform situations. In order to respond to the need for an innovative approach to curriculum development or to provide statewide exemplars of well-articulated, standards-based programs, supervisors need to take on new leadership roles and move beyond the traditional definitions of supervision.

New Resources for World Languages Supervisors

What are the most contemporary tools available to assist world language supervisors in their role as instructional leaders in the quest to strengthen teacher competence? One of the most useful tools is current research that supports the criteria for effective professional development for teachers. Sparks (2002) and Diaz-Maggoli (2004) maintain that professional development should be ongoing and embedded in the daily lives of teachers; studies show that benefits gained from one-day, how-to workshops are very limited. Unlike the fragmented workshop model, professional learning embedded in the daily work of teachers produces deep understanding, transforms existing ways of thinking, and produces a continuous stream of goal-focused actions that change teacher practice (Sparks, 2004). Several national documents, such as the *World Languages Other Than English Standards*, produced by the National Board for Professional Teaching Standards (NBPTS) (2001), also emphasize the need for continuous professional development tailored to teachers' specific needs. For the world language practitioner, those needs include discussion of language, culture, and pedagogy that calls for a differentiated approach to addressing varying knowledge and skills. For example, teachers need to maintain and update their knowledge of changing patterns in language use and cultural norms in the language they teach and include this knowledge in their instructional decisions (NBPTS, 2001).

Supervisors of world languages play a key role in supporting the professional development of individual teachers. They listen to teachers and assist them with selecting, planning, carrying out, and evaluating professional development opportunities tailored toward individual needs. Some examples of site-based, job-embedded approaches supervisors may consider in discussion with their teachers include peer coaching, teacher study groups, mentoring, professional development portfolios, and action research. Teachers also may participate in school or district networks that strengthen content knowledge and pedagogy using these approaches.

Action Research

Action research is evolving as a powerful strategy for long-term professional development in the field. Rick Donato (2003) maintains that through the action research process, "teachers investigate closely a self-selected area of interest with a view toward seeing learning in a new light and thinking in alternate ways about instruction" (p. 1). Professional growth occurs when teachers identify important instructional problems that exist in their classrooms and use action research to assist in finding solutions for these problems. This process is linked directly to teachers and takes place in their classrooms through their interactions with students. "Action research is conducted *by* teachers, not merely *on* teachers by researchers who often lack knowledge of daily life in classrooms," asserts Donato (p. 1).

What does action research look and feel like though the lens of the world language practitioner? Consider the following action research project on integrative teaching by a teacher from the Dallas (Tex.) Independent School District who focused on the following research question: What will be the effect of an interdisciplinary teaching unit on students' performance as evidenced by the end product (an original poem), on student and teacher satisfaction, and on attitudes regarding integrative teaching? (Boryczka, 2003)

The purpose of her project was twofold. She sought to learn how students would perceive and react to the professional interaction and collaboration between their Spanish teacher and her colleague, an English teacher, as they teamed to introduce a unit on poetry. Additionally, she wanted to engage the students in the development of the lesson to determine whether this procedure was effective. The evidence she gathered to support the project findings included the end student product— an ode—and a student survey and feedback form. At the close of the unit, all students in the class successfully completed an ode on a topic or theme that reflected their interest. Additionally, survey results indicated a high level of student satisfaction. Most students felt integrative teaching provided an environment that fostered collaboration while encouraging creativity and intellectual curiosity. The feedback form also indicated that most students were aware of the collaborative work with the teacher and her colleague and viewed it as important to the success of the unit. As a result of this action research project, the teacher is committed to creating units and lesson plans that provide ample opportunities for collaboration with other disciplines as well as for student involvement in selecting lesson themes and topics (Boryczka, 2003, pp. 4–5).

Library of Classroom Practices

One of the most recent resources available for professional development is the 2003 video library produced by the WGBH Educational Foundation for Annenberg/Corporation for Public Broadcasting (CPB) in conjunction with the ACTFL. The video library, entitled *Teaching Foreign Languages K–12* (Annenberg/CPB, 2003a), can be used for individual or group professional development and showcases unscripted teaching practices and student interactions in a range of classrooms. Lessons reflect standards-based instruction as well as formal and informal assessment practices. The videos can provide the foundation for the establishment of a year-long (or beyond) professional development module that enables teachers to reflect on their own teaching and try new approaches in the classroom.

The videos are lively and provocative. They are designed to inspire thoughtful discussion and reflection and to provide the opportunity to learn from the successful practices of other teachers. The language classrooms shown in this library include Spanish, French, German, Japanese, Italian, Latin, Russian, and Chinese. All classroom videos are subtitled in English and are appropriate for K–12 teachers of any world language. The library includes a 30-minute introduction and 60-minute overviews of the *ACTFL Standards for Foreign Language Learning* and new assessment practices, as well as 27 classroom programs.

Within the half-hour classroom programs, teachers from schools across the country model interpersonal, interpretive, and presentational modes of communication throughout a range of grade and competency levels. Concepts of culture, comparisons, connections to students' lives, and the importance of community also are integrated into the lessons. A Web site and print guide accompany the video programs. The programs can be viewed on the Annenberg/CPB Channel, a free satellite channel broadcast 24 hours a day, seven days a week (requires a digital satellite receiver); on the www .learner.org Web site (free on-demand viewing that requires a broadcast connection); or by purchasing the videotape collection in its entirety or in elementary, middle, or high school grade-level bands. Purchasing information can be found on the Annenberg/CPB (2003b) Learner.org Web site (www.learner.org/channel/libraries/tfl).

Because quality professional development is inextricably linked to what is happening in the classroom, to educational reform, and to best practice, the primary role of the world language supervisor is to act as a catalyst for strengthening teacher competence. Supervisors of world languages are charged with the task of creating the kinds of structures that will support the learning and teaching process in their school districts. Helene Zimmer-Loew, executive director of the American Association of Teachers of German, makes a distinction between the dos and don'ts of supervisory responsibilities. "They [supervisors] do not work in isolation, do not try to identify problems alone, do not make decisions unilaterally, and do not deal solely with the upper echelons of the school community" (2000, p. 173). Rather, they "support teachers in the use of new materials, instructional methods, and the learning process" (p. 174). Supervisors help teachers develop new ways of thinking about teaching and learning in the classroom and of observing how students are thinking and learning. They provide opportunities for teachers to reflect and discuss their teaching and assist them in identifying and recognizing the knowledge and skills necessary to improve their practice and seek new solutions. In doing so, supervisors support teachers in becoming lifelong learners about how to improve teaching and learning.

REFLECTIONS

The time is right for implementing these changes. Economic and social globalization is linking people across linguistic and cultural borders. With this in mind, language instruction needs to prepare students for encounters with people from other cultures, both today and in the future, providing them with the skills and knowledge they will need for communicating with and understanding each other more effectively. In the United States, 2005, the Year of Languages, begins a decade-long emphasis on realizing the vision of languages for all.

The ability to communicate effectively with people across languages and cultures is a critical skill in the 21st century. Many countries in Europe, Asia, and other regions of the world have embraced this belief and it is reflected in their promotion of language learning and linguistic diversity through state, regional, and national policies. For example, the European Union and its member states have set an overall goal for the teaching of at least two world languages beginning at an early age and have put into motion a variety of initiatives to meet this goal. One such initiative is the *Common European Frame-work of Reference for Languages*, developed by the Council of Europe in 2001. The framework provides a clear direction for the teaching, learning, and assessment of languages for member states in light of the overall language policy of the Council of Europe and its promotion of plurilingualism in response to the continent's linguistic and cultural diversity (Council of Europe, 2001). In Australia, due to recent waves of immigration, societal multilingualism in a variety of European, Asian, and other international languages is being encouraged (Duff, 2004). In China, according to Vice Minister of Education Zhang Xinsheng, the number of Chinese students studying English is greater than the entire U.S. population (2004). However, in the United States, it is still widely accepted that knowledge of the English language, often considered the *lingua franca* (the dominant language of international business, new technologies, and popular culture), is sufficient.

Why has this thinking not changed? In a world of multinationals and of import and export imbalances, Americans have enjoyed a position of advantage. By and large, other countries have come to us, invested with us, sold to us on our terms, and eagerly welcomed our "western" products. This attitude also has been reinforced by our geography. Our country takes up a good portion of an entire continent, and the only language needed to travel from one end to the other is English. It is no surprise, then, that learning other languages is still perceived as an intellectual exercise, certainly not a necessity, and at best an inconsistent priority depending on the international crisis of the times. Consequently, world language education has not yet been successfully implemented systemically despite the onset of globalization and the current era of education reform.

Will globalization lead to an Americanization of global culture? The likelihood appears remote that the trappings of American society will overtake the strong and vibrant cultures that exist worldwide. Will globalization lead to the global adoption of English? Despite the current dominant role played by the English-speaking world powers, speakers of English represent a very small percentage of the world's population—and this trend will continue, according to population experts (see Figure 6). The key question, then, is whether we can continue to believe that the world will interact with us in English, and whether we can continue to deny that knowledge of other languages and cultures is essential.

One of the most recent initiatives undertaken to address the need for language study and language shortfalls in the United States began with the June 2004 National Foreign Language Conference held at the University of Maryland and cosponsored by the Department of Defense and the Center for the Advanced Study of Languages. The purpose of the conference was to issue a call to action to move the nation toward a 21st century vision of language proficiency (U.S. Department of Defense, 2004):

Our vision is a world in which the United States is a stronger global leader through proficiency in foreign languages and understanding of the cultures of the world. These abilities are strengths of our public and private sectors and pillars of our educational system. The government, academic, and private sectors contribute to, and mutually benefit from these national capabilities. (p. iii)

The conference brought together key representatives from the academic, business, government, and private sectors, all of whom underscored the need for a national plan to create a more language-competent society and deliberated on a course of action to achieve these goals. Conference participants reached consensus that existing language programs, even if appropriately funded and coordinated, are not sufficient. They urged the creation of a

---

Figure 6
Top Languages Worldwide by Population

The Summer Institute for Linguistics (SIL) Ethnologue Survey (1999) lists the following as the top languages by population (number of native speakers given in parentheses). Interestingly, with the exception of Spanish, the languages most commonly offered in schools are not the most commonly spoken world languages. Almost 7 million students in American public schools are enrolled in foreign language classes in grades 7–12, according to a 2002 survey by the American Council on the Teaching of Foreign Languages. Ninety-two percent of them are studying Spanish, French, and German; only eight percent are studying other languages (National Virtual Translation Center, 2004).

1. Chinese* (937,132,000)
2. Spanish (332,000,000)
3. English (322,000,000)
4. Bengali (189,000,000)
5. Hindi/Urdu (182,000,000)
6. Arabic* (174,950,000)
7. Portuguese (170,000,000)
8. Russian (170,000,000)
9. Japanese (125,000,000)
10. German (98,000,000)
11. French* (79,572,000)

* The totals given for Chinese, Arabic, and French include more than one SIL variety.

systematic and systemic approach to foreign language education in the United States that includes

- Language instruction that begins in the earliest grades and continues with well-articulated sequences of instruction throughout the educational pipeline.

- Offerings that include languages that are central to global literacy and important for future economic and security needs.

- Maintenance and continued development of heritage-language proficiency to promote biliteracy and enhance opportunities for further achievement.

- A financial commitment to foreign language education at the federal budgetary level and by state legislatures.

- Integration of the teaching of foreign languages into the teaching of reading, writing, and other areas of accountability and the preparation of teachers to effectively do so.

- Incorporation of foreign languages into the accountability system.

- Establishment of standards-driven, reform-based policies for teaching foreign languages and cultures throughout the educational pipeline.

- Recruitment of qualified teachers and enhancement of teacher capacity for teaching excellence through preservice education, professional development, and opportunities for exchange and study abroad.

- Development of policy and legislation to address gaps in national language capacity, taking into account our existing sociolinguistic reality, recognizing language rights, and promoting pluriculturalism and multilingualism.

- Establishment of a national coordinating entity to develop, organize, and oversee the implementation of a national foreign language strategy that will provide U.S. students with the kinds of instructional programs needed to acquire meaningful levels of language competence. (U.S. Department of Defense, 2004)

The Year of Languages

Under the auspices of the American Council on the Teaching of Foreign Languages, 2005 has been designated as the Year of Languages. The goals of the observance in the United States are to build public awareness of the value of language learning, facilitate dialogue between education leaders and policymakers, and encourage and support research on language learning. This ambitious initiative represents the most coordinated collaboration of educators at the local, state, regional, and national levels that has ever taken place in the language profession. Business groups and international economic councils, chambers of commerce in the United States, U.S. embassies abroad, foreign consulates and embassies in the United States, and international governments will participate in a variety of activities in support of the goals of this initiative.

Their efforts will focus on highlighting the integral role of languages in school, work, and business environments of the 21st century, providing Americans with a new and fresh perspective on the value of learning other languages. The hope behind the initiative is that the Year of Languages will be the launching pad for many future language activities and initiatives that will take place in the United States over the next decade.

The Year of Languages in the United States parallels events and celebrations that already have taken place in other parts of the world. The year 2001 was designated the Year of Languages in Europe and, since that time, Europeans have been celebrating one week of language promotion every year. The year 2006 has been designated the Year of Languages in China, and Chinese citizens are reportedly excited about the opportunity to learn additional languages to prepare for the 2008 Olympics, set to be held in Beijing (ACTFL, 2004).

A Renewed Focus on International Education

In 2001, the National Commission on Asia in the Schools released the report *Asia in the Schools: Preparing Young Americans for Today's Interconnected World*. The report concluded that American students had rudimentary knowledge about global issues and cultures. In addition, the report emphasized that language instruction did not reflect the realities of the interconnected world of the 21st century—a world that requires individuals to be proficient in *current* major world languages. Moreover, very few American high school or college students graduate with the level of proficiency needed to successfully interact in a culturally appropriate manner with peoples from other cultures. Subsequent to the release of this report, the Asia Society formed the National Coalition on Asia and International Studies in the Schools. The goal of the coalition is to take actions to address the international knowledge gap in our schools.

One of its major initiatives has been the creation of annual States Institutes to assist states in addressing the question of how to improve student knowledge and skills about other regions of the world, their languages, and their cultures. At the first States Institute, in 2002, state leaders reached consensus that international knowledge and skills are essential not only for individual states and local communities, but also for the nation as a whole because of the effect on the economy and jobs, human and national security, social and cultural integration, and humanitarian responses to human need (Castaing, 2002, p. 8). Viewed in this way, the acquisition of world languages plays a key role in achieving the goals of international education. Every important issue that is international in scope involves interaction with other cultures, the success

of which depends on the ability of our schools to produce linguistic and culturally proficient speakers of languages other than English. The 2002 report further cites model programs in world languages for higher education, heritage-language speakers, and those using business-language resources and technology. Further, it poses questions for state and local policymakers to consider regarding world language programs. To strengthen world languages on the district level, for example, some of the questions supervisors, world language teachers, curriculum coordinators, and policymakers might reflect upon include the following:

- What are our goals in teaching world languages? What should they be?

- Do all students have the opportunity to learn a second language, *including* a current major world language?

- What percentage of the student population studies a world language? How many complete a sequence of four or more years of study? How many attain proficiency beyond the intermediate-low level on the *ACTFL K–12 Performance Guidelines*?

- Are there programs designed specifically for heritage-language speakers? Is technology used in any way to assist with language instruction or as an instructional alternative for the less commonly taught languages?

- What local incentives could be put in place to expand the K–12 study of world languages?

The changes required to close the international knowledge gap are substantial and incorporate reform of the nation's implicit policies and current practices in world language education. The National Coalition of Asia and International Education is working in collaboration with national language organizations and policymakers to achieve these goals. It is hopeful that these efforts will lead to the development of a national strategy consisting of plans and policies that engage the American public in a way that elicits support for actions that address the significant gaps in our national language capabilities—gaps that continue to undermine cross-cultural communication and understanding both at home and abroad.

Local Advocacy

The initiatives described above share a common commitment to the development of national language and cultural capabilities and to moving the nation forward in producing globally literate citizens. Teachers and supervisors of world languages can support these efforts at the local level. Many educators may not realize that their actions can affect the way decisions pertaining to world language education are made at the local or state levels. Figure 7 offers several strategies world language teachers and supervisors can use to influence the creation of policies in support of quality second-language education.

WORKS CITED

Allen, L. Q. (1999). Designing curriculum for standards-based culture/language learning. *Northeast Conference Review, 47,* 14–21.

American Council on the Teaching of Foreign Languages. (1999). *ACTFL performance guidelines for K–12 learners.* Yonkers, NY: Author.

American Council on the Teaching of Foreign Languages. (2004). *2005: The year of languages.* Retrieved April 26, 2005, from www.actfl.org/i4a/pages/index.cfm?pageid=3422

Annenberg/CPB. (2003a). *Teaching foreign languages K–12: A library of classroom practices.* [Pamphlet]. Boston: WGBH Educational Foundation in conjunction with the American Council on the Teaching of Foreign Languages.

Annenberg/CPB. (2003b). *Teaching foreign languages K–12: A library of classroom practices.* Retrieved April 26, 2005, from www.learner.org/channel/libraries/tfl

Boryczka, C. (2003). Integrative teaching. In E. Phillips (Ed.), *LOTE CED Communiqué, 8,* 4–5.

Caine, R. N., & Caine, G. (1997). *Education on the edge of possibility.* Alexandria, VA: Association for Supervision and Curriculum Development.

Castaing, M. (2002, November). *States institute on international education in the schools: Institute report.* New York: The Asia Society.

Center for Advanced Research on Language Acquisition. (2003). *Minnesota language proficiency assessments.* Minneapolis: University of Minnesota.

Center for Applied Linguistics. (2004). *Ñandutí: Early foreign language learning: Foreign language advocacy.* Retrieved April 26, 2005, from www.cal.org/earlylang/faadvc.htm

Clementi, D. (2004, September 27). *World languages: Communicating important ideas.* Workshop presented for the New Jersey Department of Education in Monroe Township, N.J.

Council of Chief State School Officers. (2004). *Surveys of enacted curriculum.* Washington, DC: CCSSO. Retrieved April 26, 2005, from www.ccsso.org/projects/Surveys_of_Enacted_Curriculum

Council of Europe. (2001). *A common European framework of reference for languages.* Retrieved April 26, 2005, from www.culture2.coe.int/portfolio/documents_intro/common_framework.html

Curtain, H. (April 1995). Integrating foreign language and content instruction in grades K–8. *ERIC Digest.* Washington, DC: ERIC Clearinghouse on Languages and Linguistics.

Curtain, H., & Dahlberg, C. A. (2004). *Key concepts for success: Elementary and middle school foreign languages.* Boston: Pearson Education, Inc.

Curtain, H., & Pesola, C. A. (1994). *Languages and children, making the match: Foreign language instruction for an early start, grades K–8.* Boston: Pearson Education, Inc.

Doggett, G. (2003). The communicative approach. *CAL Digest Series 1: Complete Collection.* Washington, DC: Center for Applied Linguistics.

Figure 7
Eight Influential Strategies for World Language Advocacy

1. **Stay updated about political issues** affecting language education at the local, state, and national levels. *Example:* Check media outlets, such as Web sites, television coverage, and news reports of educational issues.

2. **Prioritize issues** that your state foreign language association should address concerning policy and budget decisions that may affect language education. *Example:* How will changes in the district boundaries affect the population demographics of your school? How might the allocation of school funds to other program areas or the reduction of overall school funding affect program implementations? Share this information with the relevant stakeholders in your area.

3. **Earmark specific points** in the decision-making process where advocacy efforts will have the greatest effect along with persons in relevant decision-making positions. *Example:* Get to know the movers and shakers on the board and in the community who are concerned about decisions that will have an impact maintaining program quality, such as when administrators propose time allocation reductions in an elementary program.

4. **Inform** all education stakeholders about these issues and your activities through newsletters, alerts, and any other media that reaches your constituency. *Example:* Create a Web site to inform people about issues in your community. Update it frequently to make sure the information remains current.

5. **Connect with the media** via letters to the editor, op-ed pieces, and radio and TV segments. *Example:* Invite local media to cover your meetings, activities, and events that showcase what students have learned in the program. Consider writing an op-ed piece for a journal or other publication outlining your position.

6. **Form alliances** with other organizations and key constituency groups. *Example:* Work with educators at multiple levels in your community to develop coordinated plans of instruction. Talk with parent–teacher organizations, as well, to share information.

7. **Be clear** about all aspects of your foreign language budget with "bottom line" justification. *Example:* Recognize that good programs cost money and be honest about it, but be sure to point out that the benefits for students are immeasurable.

8. **Establish and maintain an active network** of people who promise to participate in the above activities. *Example:* Network with friends and colleagues. Assign responsibilities so all aspects of a program are covered and represented. Alumni organizations, blogs, listservs, and online postings can help as well.

Doggett, G. (2003, January). Eight approaches to language learning. *CAL Digest Series 1: Complete Collection.* Washington, DC: Center for Applied Linguistics.

Diaz-Maggoli, G. (2004). *A passion for learning: Teacher-centered professional development.* Alexandria, VA: Association for Supervision and Curriculum Development.

Donato, R. (2000). Building knowledge, building leaders: Collaborating for research and change. In L. M. Wallinger (Ed.), *Teaching in changing times: The courage to lead.* (Northeast Conference Reports, pp. 89–119). New York: McGraw-Hill Higher Education.

Donato, R. (2003, May). Action Research: Reseeing learning and rethinking practice in the LOTE classroom. In E. Phillips (Ed.), *LOTE CED Communiqué, 8,* 1–2.

Duff, P. (2004, January 12–14). *Foreign language policies, research, and educational possibilities: A western perspective.* Paper presented at the APEC Educational Summit in Beijing.

Fullan, M. (2002). The change leader. *Educational Leadership, 59*(8), 16–20.

Galloway, V. (1999). Bridges and boundaries: Growing the cross-cultural mind. In M. A. Kassen & M. G. Abbott (Eds.), *Language learners of tomorrow: Process and promise* (151–185). Lincolnwood, IL: National Textbook Company.

Genesee, F., & Cloud, N. (1998, March). Multilingualism is basic. *Educational Leadership, 55*(6), 62–65.

Gilzow, D. F., & Branaman, L. E. (2000). *Lessons learned: Model foreign language programs.* Washington, DC: The Center for Applied Linguistics and Delta Systems.

Internet World Stats. (2005). Internet users by language. Retrieved April 1, 2005, from www .internetworldstats.com/stats7.htm

Jensen, J. (2002). Supervisors as agents of change: Creating innovative structures to support teaching and learning. *New Jersey Journal of Supervision and Curriculum Development, 46,* (43–68).

Jensen, J. (2004). [Informal electronic survey of the National Council of State Supervisors for Languages]. Unpublished raw data.

Kennedy, T. J. (1999, Spring). GLOBE integrates mathematics, science, social studies, and technology into the foreign language classroom. *Learning Languages, 4*(3), 23–25.

Kennedy, T. J. (2003, Spring). Making content connections through foreign language instruction via GLOBE. *ERIC/CLL News Bulletin, 26*(2). Washington, DC: ERIC Clearinghouse on Languages and Linguistics.

Kennedy, T. J., & Canney, G. (2000). Collaborating across language, age, and geographic borders. In K. Risko & K. Bromley (Eds.), *Collaboration for diverse learners: Viewpoints and practices* (pp. 310–329). Newark, DE: International Reading Association.

Kenyon, D., Farr, B., Mitchell, J., & Armengol, R. (2000). *Framework for the 2004 foreign language national assessment of educational progress.* Washington, DC: National Assessment Governing Board.

Krashen, S. D. (1982). *Principles and practice in second language acquisition.* Oxford: Pergamon Press.

Kubota, R. (1999). Learning Japanese via satellite in an American high school: A case study. *Foreign Language Annals, 32*(3), 329–347.

Language Learning Solutions. (2003). *Standards-based measurement of proficiency.* Retrieved April 26, 2005, from www.onlinells.com/onlinells/stamp.asp

Little, D., & Perclová, R. (2002). *The European language portfolio: A guide for teachers and teacher trainers.* Council of Europe: Strasbourg, France.

Moeller, A., Scow, V., & Van Houten, J. B. (2005). Documenting and improving student learning through linguafolios. In P. Boyles & P. Sandrock, Eds., *The year of languages: challenges, changes, and choices.* Milwaukee, WI: Central States Conference on the Teaching of Foreign Languages.

National Association of District Supervisors of Foreign Languages. (1999). *Characteristics of effective foreign language instruction.* Retrieved April 26, 2005, from www.nadsfl.org/characteristics

National Association of District Supervisors of Foreign Languages. (n.d.). *The language supervisor: An indispensable part of a quality language program.* Retrieved April 26, 2005, from www.nadsfl.org/qualityprogram

National Board for Professional Teaching Standards. (2001). *Standards for languages other than English.* Washington, DC: Author.

National Standards in Foreign Language Education Project. (1996). *Standards for foreign language learning: Preparing for the 21st century.* Yonkers, NY: Author.

National Standards in Foreign Language Education Project. (1999). *Standards for foreign language learning in the 21st century.* Lawrence, KS: Allen Press, Inc.

National Virtual Translation Center. (2004). *Languages of the world.* Retrieved April 26, 2005, from www.nvtc .gov/lotw/months/november/USschoollanguages.htm

Rhodes, N., & Pufahl, I. (2004). *Language by video: An overview of foreign language instructional videos for children.* Washington, DC: Center for Applied Linguistics.

Sandrock, P. (2002). *Planning curriculum for learning world languages.* Madison, WI: Wisconsin Department of Public Instruction.

Social Science Education Consortium. (1999). *Culture in the foreign language classroom: A survey of high school teachers' practices and needs (final report).* Boulder, CO: Author.

Sparks, D. (2002). *Designing powerful staff development for teachers and principals.* Oxford, OH: National Staff Development Council.

Sparks, D. (2004, August 11). *Leading for results: Transforming teaching, learning and relationships in schools.* Presentation given to the New Jersey Professional Teachers Standards Board.

Spinelli, E., & Nerenz, A. G. (2004, Spring). Learning scenarios: The new foreign language curriculum. *CLEAR News, 8*(1), 1–6.

Sprenger, M. (1999). *Learning & memory: The brain in action.* Alexandria, VA: Association for Supervision and Curriculum Development.

Thomas, W., & Collier, V. (1997). School effectiveness for language minority students. *NCBE Resource Collection Series Number 9.* Washington, DC: National Clearinghouse for Bilingual Education.

U.S. Department of Defense. (2004): *A call to action for national foreign language capabilities.* Draft white paper. Washington, DC: Author.

Webb, E., & Sandrock, P. (2003). *Learning languages in middle schools.* National Council of State Supervisors of Foreign Languages. Retrieved April 1, 2005, from www.ncssfl.org/papers/FinalMiddleSchool.pdf

Wiggins, G., & McTighe, J. (1998). *Understanding by design.* Alexandria, VA: Association for Supervision and Curriculum Development.

Wolfe, P. (2001). *Brain matters: Translating research into classroom practice.* Alexandria, VA: Association for Supervision and Curriculum Development.

Xinsheng, Z. (2004, July 19). Keynote speech delivered at The College Board in New York.

Zimmer-Loew, H. (2000). Professional development and change. In R. M. Terry & F. W. Medley (Eds.), *Agents of change in a changing age* (169–209). Lincolnwood, IL: National Textbook Company.

III. QUESTIONS AND ANSWERS

The following questions and answers focus on strategies that can overcome what are often perceived as common barriers to implementing effective world language programs.

1. *How can my district adapt world languages instruction to meet the needs of diverse learners?*

Let's first identify what we mean by the term "diverse learners" in today's world language classroom. For the purposes of this document, diverse learners are students whose learning characteristics and styles may require alternative instructional strategies to ensure they have a successful second-language learning experience and maximize their second-language learning potential. Diverse learners typically meet curricular goals and objectives at varying levels of intensity or degrees of sophistication and according to different timetables; thus, "differentiating the curriculum" refers to adjustments in content, teaching strategies, expectations of student mastery, and scope and sequence. Varying learning capabilities, learning needs, and learning styles have specific implications for instructional strategies in the world language classroom.

Diverse learners may be addressed in different categories:

- Students with diverse talents (multiple intelligences)

- Students with high abilities (exceptionally able)

- Students with disabilities (special education)

- Students who are English language learners (heritage-language learners)

Students with Diverse Talents (Multiple Intelligences)

The importance of varying instructional strategies in the world language classroom is supported by the work of Howard Gardner (1983), who maintains that each student has a dominant learning style that is a unique combination of the types of intelligences the student possesses. Most adaptations that meet the needs of varying learning styles are beneficial to all learners and add variety and interest to class activities. Additionally, a variety of instructional activities and products may be categorized for each level of thinking based on Bloom's taxonomy (knowledge, comprehension, application, analysis, synthesis, evaluation). By designing a variety of activities that require different levels of thinking, teachers provide appropriate opportunities for diverse students whose intelligences range across the spectrum. Figure 8 gives examples of such activities according to their corresponding category of Bloom's taxonomy.

For the most part, the world language profession has not been responsive to the second-language needs of students enrolled in vocational-technical programs, many of whom possess strong kinesthetic intelligence. Introductory language courses offered in some vocational-technical programs most often do not appeal to these students, whose area of interest is highly focused on their particular program (e.g., culinary arts, auto mechanics, or health-related occupations). However, community colleges across the country are introducing an interesting model for consideration; they are beginning to change language course offerings to meet the needs of police officers, firefighters, health workers, and those in service professions who require job-specific language or needs-based language to assist them (Gifford, 2004). Such programs, referred to as *occupational language programs*, include cross-cultural training designed to eliminate misunderstandings that arise in the workplace between English-dominant speakers and speakers of languages other than English. Instructors use nontraditional learning strategies, with a focus on comprehension and oral production of a limited repertoire of conversational

Figure 8
World Languages and Bloom's Taxonomy

Knowledge/ Comprehension	Application	Analysis	Synthesis	Evaluation
What students will do:	*What students will do:*	*What students will do:*	*What students will do:*	*What students will do:*
• Arrange lines of dialogue. • Fill out authentic forms from the target country. • Listen for sequence. • Explain the "What? Who? Where? How? Why?" • Give a description of scenes from a video presentation. • Describe pictures from the target country. • Define words. • Listen and paraphrase in English a conversation heard in the target language. • Draw a picture from a verbal description of a scene or object in the target culture.	• Dub cartoons or TV shows. • Command others to perform an activity step by step. • Apply a cultural custom to a real-life situation in the target country. • Interview class-mates about their daily activities. • Make shopping lists and plan menus for various cultural or social events. • Apply rules of correct cultural protocol while dining in the target country. • Classify words, poems, authentic materials, or genres. • Apply gestures learned to an authentic situation. • Apply reading strategies to understand authentic texts.	• Identify elements of a particular literary form. • Analyze the lyrics of popular songs to compare both cultures' perspectives. • Compare points of view found in two editorials. • Analyze stories, poems, and other authentic materials. • Analyze a scene in the target culture from a play or TV show. • Find evidence to support an opinion. • Compare students' customs with those of the target culture. • Conduct a survey and analyze the results. • Identify the best route to a historic site in the target country. • Play the role of a tourist who bargains for merchandise in the target country.	• Write an alternative ending to a story. • Hypothesize consequences if historical events had ended differently. • Write titles for a play, story, or article. • Write headlines in newspaper style on current issues in the target country. • Predict future events. • Write a diary of an imaginary trip. • Extend a story. • Hypothesize the reaction to different situations based on cultural beliefs. • Compose a poem, skit, role-play scenario, or advertisement. • Create hypothetical real-world situations found in the target culture. • Create an infomercial.	• Prioritize solutions to cultural dilemmas. • Express and justify opinions on creative products of the culture. • Give and support opinions about issues. • Evaluate TV shows, movies, cartoons, articles in the media, or presentations. • Write an editorial giving and supporting an opinion. • Express the pros and cons of policies. • Give and support a decision in a mock trial. • Write to an appropriate official in the target country with suggestions for the resolution of a real-world problem. • Justify a list of sites to visit in the target country. • Read an editorial in a target-country newspaper and send a response. • Evaluate best Web pages for sources of current events in the target country.

Source: From *Nebraska K–12 Foreign Language Frameworks* (p. 307), 1996, Lincoln, NE: Nebraska Department of Education. Copyright 1996 by the Nebraska Department of Education. Adapted with permission.

words and phrases. At the secondary level, as well, this model may be of particular interest for students who are not motivated to intensely study a second language that holds little academic interest for them. Because the primary goal of these programs is to equip learners to perform routine job functions in the target language—thereby providing an immediate application of what is being studied—motivation to learn a language is strong and viewed as a practical skill for the workplace.

Students with High Abilities (Exceptionally Able/Gifted)

Of all of the groups of diverse learners, exceptionally able learners often are among the most underserved in the world language classroom, particularly at beginning levels of instruction. Exceptionally able students often demonstrate a high degree of intellectual, creative, or artistic ability and can grasp concepts rapidly or intuitively. Just as in other

content areas, these students may need accommodations or special instruction to achieve at levels commensurate with their abilities. Once properly identified, exceptional students should be provided with appropriate instructional accommodations that are integrated into world language instruction at all levels. Figure 9 provides examples of specific adaptation strategies for the world languages classroom.

Students with Disabilities (Special Education)

Adaptations provide students with disabilities the opportunity to maximize their strengths and compensate for their learning differences. Certain adaptations structure students' learning in a more explicit, systematic way, whereas others provide alternative means for students to acquire or demonstrate their knowledge. Most adaptations used in the world language classroom are based on effective instructional practices that benefit all students, but are essential for a student with disabilities. Students

---

Figure 9
Suggested Adaptation Strategies for Exceptionally Able
and Gifted Learners in the World Language Classroom

Student adaptations may include, but are not limited to, the following:

- Researching and discussing cultural issues or perspectives in more depth.
- Posing questions that involve inferencing and focus on complex cross-curricular themes or global problems.
- Explaining reasons for taking a certain position or making a specific decision, both orally and in writing in the target language.
- Creating original songs, stories, short plays, poems, and designs that show multicultural perspectives of a specific theme or have a futuristic twist.
- Being held accountable for additional authentic interpretive listening tasks.
- Creating experiences and performances that reflect the results of research, interviews, or surveys in the target language.
- Retelling a story or experience from other content areas in the target language.
- Writing editorials and letters to target-language newspapers in the United States.
- E-mailing articles, commentaries, or reviews to target-culture schools, publications, organizations, newspapers, or magazines.
- Handling assignments involving more sophisticated computer research and reporting in the target language.
- Interpreting assignments such as handouts or information for Web searches in the target language.
- Processing a greater volume of any given print material.
- Independently choosing world language projects.

Source: From *New Jersey World Languages Curriculum Framework* (p. 218), 1999, Trenton, NJ: New Jersey Department of Education. Copyright 1999 by the New Jersey Department of Education. Reprinted with permission.

with disabilities often require adaptations that fall into four categories: instructional preparation, instructional prompts, instructional application, and instructional monitoring.

Instructional preparation refers to how information is structured and organized. Examples of instructional preparation techniques include preteaching vocabulary (meaning and pronunciation); using visual demonstrations, illustrations, and models; presenting mini-lessons; using brainstorming and webbing; and relating to personal experiences. *Instructional prompts* activate recall, generate classification, cue associations and connections, and highlight and clarify essential concepts. Examples of instructional prompts include graphic and semantic organizers, mnemonic devices, movement cues, manipulatives, and scaffolding. The purpose of *instructional application* is to simplify abstract concepts and provide concrete examples, build connections and associations, engage multiple modalities, and relate to everyday experiences. Examples include hands-on activities; dramatization, music, or movement; drawing or painting; games; and structured dialogue. *Instructional monitoring* techniques provide for continuous checks for understanding, promote participation, provide reinforcement and feedback, and develop self-questioning and self-regulation. Examples of these techniques are vocabulary journals, portfolios, peer reviews, self-monitoring checklists, and student "think-alouds."

Students with disabilities also may require specific adaptations for instructional groupings (peer partners and buddy systems), an instructional support person, special seating arrangements, and adaptive equipment and materials. In terms of assessment, these students need to be provided with a wide range of tasks to demonstrate their knowledge and skills, some of which may require extended time and a preferred response mode (e.g., illustrated, modeled, oral). Grading practices also may need to be modified (e.g., use of a student portfolio that shows mastery of certain skills and progress over the continuum, rather than letter grades).

Although some students with disabilities are eager to engage in various world language activities, others are not; this may be due to a variety of factors, some of which may be related to their individual disabilities. Motivational strategies therefore become important tools to assist students in becoming successfully involved in world language activities. Such strategies include a choice of activities; hands-on, multimodal activities; doable learner tasks; modification of activities to meet different learning styles; student involvement in goal-setting and assessment activities; and the option of working with others or alone. Figure 10 provides concrete examples of strategies for meeting specific learning needs in skill and instructional areas. Although they are grouped to address specific kinds of learning needs, the strategies may be beneficial to other students in the same classroom.

Students Who Are English Language Learners (Heritage-Language Learners)

Students who arrive in classrooms with diverse levels of English-language proficiency should be given the same opportunity as others to learn world languages. In the best-case scenario, they should be provided with opportunities to maintain and develop native language skills and also to study another world language in addition to English at some point in their schooling. A relatively new term—heritage-language learners—is used in practice to describe students with varying levels of native-language proficiency. According to Guadalupe Valdes, Stanford University professor and recognized expert on heritage-language learners, a heritage-language learner is "a language student who is raised in a home where a non-English language is spoken, who speaks or at least understands the language, and who is to some degree bilingual in that language and in English" (2001, p. 38).

Figure 10
Considerations for Meeting Specific Learning Needs in Skill and Instructional Areas

To ensure success with speaking . . .

• Give sentence starters.
• Use graphic organizers to organize ideas and relationships.
• Use visuals.
• Allow extra response time for processing.
• Use cues and prompts to help the student know when to speak.
• Use partners.
• Phrase questions with choices embedded in them.
• Use choral reading or speaking.
• Use rhythm or music.
• Allow practice opportunities for speaking.
• Practice role-playing activities.

To ensure success with reading . . .

• Use prereading and postreading activities to preteach or reinforce main ideas.
• Use specific strategies before, during, and after reading. For example, use preview questions before, pausing to reflect during, self-evaluation and summary after.
• Provide advanced organizers when showing videos.
• Use peer tutoring.
• Provide audiotaped materials (text or study guides).
• Teach self-questioning.
• Paraphrase key points or have students paraphrase key points.
• Summarize key points or have students summarize key points.
• Label main ideas.
• Label the 5 Ws—Who? What? When? Where? Why?
• Allow highlighting of texts, passages, key words, or concepts.
• Use visual imagery.
• Explain idioms that appear in reading passages.
• Allow silent prereading.
• Allow partner reading.
• Use computer programs or games.
• Allow students to quietly read aloud (subvocalization).
• Use graphic organizers.
• Use preparatory set (i.e., talk through what a reading passage is about using new vocabulary and concepts).

To ensure success with writing . . .

• Shorten writing assignments.
• Require lists instead of sentences.
• Allow students to dictate ideas to peers.
• Provide note takers.
• Allow students to use a tape recorder to dictate writing.
• Allow visual representation of ideas.
• Provide a fill-in-the-blank form for note taking.
• Allow students to use a computer for outlining, word processing, spelling, and grammar checks.
• Provide a structure for the writing.
• Allow collaborative writing.
• Provide a model of the writing.

(continued on next page)

Figure 10 (*continued*)
Considerations for Meeting Specific Learning Needs in Skill and Instructional Areas

- Allow use of different writing utensils and paper.
- Use a flow chart for organizing ideas before the student writes.
- Brainstorm a bank of possible words that might be needed prior to the writing activity.
- Narrow the choice of topics.
- Grade on the basis of content; do not penalize for errors in mechanics and grammar.
- Allow options with a manuscript, such as cursive or keyboarding.
- Allow different positions or surfaces for writing.

To ensure success with assessment . . .

- Use a variety of authentic assessments.
- Establish criteria and expectations prior to instruction.
- Teach test-taking strategies.
- Teach the format of an upcoming test.
- Allow adequate time for test taking.
- Allow paper-and-pencil tests to be taken in a different space.
- Allow a variety of ways to respond (e.g., orally, pictorially, tape recordings).
- Give choices.
- Assess learning continuously over time, not just at the end of a unit of study.
- Use rubrics.
- Use self-assessment tools.

To ensure success when working in groups . . .

- Teach group rules and expectations.
- Teach skills of independence (e.g., bridging phrases, disagreeing agreeably, voice level).
- Teach manageable strategies for moving in and out of groups within the classroom setting.
- Post rules and expectations.
- Give adequate time, but not "fooling around" time.
- Be in close proximity to groups as they work.
- Teach students to self-monitor group progress.
- Assign student roles or responsibilities in the group.
- Teach a signal for getting the attention of all groups.
- Practice and assess students' behaviors in small-group settings.
- Use cooperative learning strategies.
- Use a wide variety of groupings (e.g., flexible, cluster, skill).

Source: From *Nebraska K–12 Foreign Language Frameworks* (pp. 302–305), 1996, Lincoln, NE: Nebraska Department of Education. Copyright 1996 by the Nebraska Department of Education. Adapted with permission.

When referring to students who fall into this description, schools have used terms such as English as a second language (ESL) students, bilingual education (BE) students, limited English proficient (LEP) students, or English language learners (ELL). These students may be able to understand spoken language but are unable to speak beyond words and phrases. Others can speak the language fluently but cannot express themselves in writing. Some can understand and speak the language well but have limited reading and writing skills due to lack of a formal education in their native countries. Finally, there are those students who can function at a high level in all language skill areas.

What implication does this diverse population of heritage-language students have for world language instruction? Simply stated, world language teachers need to know and understand their students in order to meet their varying learning needs. In addition to students' linguistic capabilities, teachers need to have information about each student's background and interests in order to tap into their talents and skills. This goes beyond the goal of having heritage-language students participating in advanced placement language courses. The ultimate goal of instruction for these students should be to speak and write effectively in an occupational or professional setting. Moreover, individuals with high levels of proficiency in a heritage language are in great demand by the academic, business, private, and government sectors.

Teachers often have difficulty working with heritage-language students in world language classes with monolingual students. This issue is addressed by various experts in a volume titled *Spanish for Native Speakers*, part of a professional development series produced by the American Association of Teachers of Spanish and Portuguese. The essence of this response seems appropriate for any language class with heritage and English-dominant students and is not applicable only to Spanish. "Ideally, mixed classes should not exist because they are pedagogically unsound. Heritage speakers of Spanish should be in SNS (Spanish for Native Speakers) courses that address their specific needs" (Samaniego & Pino, 2000, p. 32). Samaniego and Pino further acknowledge that courses for native speakers often are not found for a variety of reasons and advise teachers to challenge these students from the first day of class so they will not lose their motivation to study the language.

Motivational needs of heritage speakers are very similar to the needs of all foreign language learners. For example, students get bored very quickly if the material is too advanced or too easy, if the material is not relevant to their daily life, if there is too much direct error correction, and so forth. It is not at all surprising that native speakers have shown little motivation in the past in classes where the texts used were designed for monolingual students, did not address any of the heritage speakers' linguistic needs, and where these students were constantly being put down for not showing interest in subject matter far too simplistic for their linguistic levels. Therefore, to motivate these students, it is important that the course content address the linguistic needs of the students and provide appropriate cultural and literary readings. Teachers must always respect the language heritage speakers bring to the class, putting emphasis on alternative ways of saying things rather than insisting on eliminating community and family language patterns. (p. 36)

The following are some additional options for heritage-language students when considering the study of a world language:

Study of a world language other than English and other than the heritage language. Students may elect to study any world language in addition to English offered in the school district's world language program.

Further study of the heritage language. Students may continue to develop and enhance their native language in either a program designed specifically for native speakers of a particular language or in an out-of-school program if that language is not taught in the public school district. For example, in New Jersey, legislation requires that the Department of Education establish a World Languages Instruction Committee to develop a plan that provides students in public schools the opportunity to receive instruction in and graduation credit for a world language not taught in the district. In compliance with this law, the department established a committee that has developed an implementation plan to be followed by districts, upon the written request of a student and that student's parent(s), that grants graduation credit for a language program offered by an external organization. An external organization is defined as a nonprofit organization such as a church or community group. The committee also has developed procedures for external organizations to follow that seek district approval for their world languages programs. These procedures provide a uniform template that districts and external organizations follow to ensure credit is properly awarded to students (New Jersey Department of Education, 2004).

Satisfy requirements with the heritage language. Students may use their native language to satisfy a district or state high school language requirement when entering the 9th grade or at subsequent grade levels as newly arrived students from their native countries. Many, but not all, students who have been speaking, reading, and writing in their native language since a very young age and throughout their prior educational experience may have high proficiency levels in their native language that will satisfy requirements. This can be documented with proficiency testing.

2. What criteria should a district use to determine which languages to include in their world language program?

Language learning provides a useful tool for meeting the demands of contemporary life; when viewed in this way, the study of one or more world languages will benefit students. Moreover, students can benefit from the study of any language when it is taught with a focus on meaningful, real-life language use and in long, well-articulated sequences of instruction. Some criteria for consideration include the following:

Community interest. Parental input and the cultural heritage of the community, as well as its changing demographics, should be considered. As communities vary, so will their program offerings. The creation of dual-language/dual-immersion programs is an excellent way of capitalizing on the lan-

guages spoken in the community and of coalescing previously disconnected groups of children in a school. It is also a means of taking advantage of available resources such as staffing, materials, and existing programs within a district.

Potential for articulation. It is important that districts decide which languages will be offered at the elementary and middle school levels in order to provide continuous language instruction through high school. Long-range planning and ongoing evaluation of program articulation are necessary to ensure an effective world language program.

Availability of qualified teachers and instructional materials. This includes existing district world languages staff, classroom teachers who have high levels of proficiency in a world language, and cross-district collaboration, as well as language-specific materials to support a quality program.

Languages most frequently spoken in the world community. It is important that students have a proficiency in critical-need languages and cultures currently playing dominant roles in global affairs. Because of their level of difficulty, many of the most commonly spoken languages in the world today—such as Chinese and Hindi—require more time to achieve usable proficiency. However, these languages reflect the needs of the 21st century and are in demand in many of the diverse communities that exist throughout the country in various business and government sectors. Attaining high levels of proficiency in globally dominant languages affords students an added advantage as they seek future employment opportunities.

3. How can my district find qualified world language teachers?

To deliver the kind of instruction that helps students develop true proficiency in using the target language, a teacher needs to have a high degree of skill herself in using the language, regardless of the level being taught. The language teacher at the beginning level(s)—whether the program begins in the elementary grades, middle school grades, or senior high—sets an expectation for students regarding the nature of learning a language. If the experience is mainly one of talking about the language in English or is simply a program meant to teach some words and cultural holidays, students will not acquire useful language-learning habits. At the beginning level, students will learn the new language better if they use it to learn important content. A balance of communication modes is also critical, so that students don't come to expect that language classes will focus only on listening and speaking. Teachers must help students who already have literacy skills in their first language to tap into those skills in learning other languages.

Policymakers wanting to encourage this type of language-learning experience need to establish a state or district minimum standard for the oral proficiency of any language teacher. Several state education agencies have set a minimum standard for that oral proficiency. Such states have selected a benchmark from the oral proficiency guidelines established by ACTFL, targeting either the intermediate-high or advanced-low level for initial certification. The National Council for the Accreditation of Teacher Education (NCATE) has identified advanced-low as the minimum oral proficiency to require of future language teachers. Many states also require a period of immersion in the culture through time spent studying, living, or working abroad. This immersion requirement could also be met through domestic experiences, using the target language to a degree similar to that needed when living abroad by interacting with native speakers of the language. Such immersion requirements provide the prospective teacher with first-hand knowledge of the target culture as well as the confidence of having successfully interacted with native speakers.

Recruiting Highly Qualified Language Teachers

Having established this necessary standard for language instructors, school administrators are tasked with finding such highly qualified teachers. Recruitment efforts are not solely the realm of administrators; professional organizations also need to get involved.

Recruiting students from high school and university programs. Professional organizations, such as those serving language teachers or directors of instruction, have become proactive in bringing potential future teachers into the activities of their organizations. Numerous state organizations of world language teachers have set up programs in which high school language teachers bring students to their state conventions. To provide role models and create interest in considering language teaching as a career, convention planners have organized special workshops for the guest high school students, where recently graduated teachers share their language learning experiences and tell why and how they became language teachers. Special recognition events welcome the high school students into the profession. For university students, several state language teachers' organizations provide scholarships to subsidize the cost of attending their state conventions and again provide special workshops or events to answer the questions of these future teachers, as well as begin a network for ongoing support as they go through student teaching or first years of employment.

Recruiting from an international pool. Several state education agencies have entered into memoranda of understanding with the education offices of foreign embassies, with the prime goal of encouraging foreign teachers to serve as language teachers in the state. Whether arranged through a third party, such as Visiting International Faculty, Inc. (N.C.), or through the state education agency, these efforts have resulted in hundreds of foreign teachers helping to relieve the shortage of language teachers in certain states. Texas employs more than 300 foreign teachers to fill such vacancies; North Carolina employs more than 50. These efforts are not meant to replace U.S. citizens in these positions, but are helpful to districts that have been unable to fill certain language teaching jobs. The teacher from abroad brings native language and culture to the school and also benefits the nonnative-speaking teachers in the district. The foreign teachers and the U.S. teachers learn from each other; the foreign teachers share their language and culture, and the U.S. teachers share teaching strategies successful in American schools.

Recruiting heritage speakers. Heritage speakers are people already in the United States with some proficiency in the language of their heritage; however, the proficiency may range from very limited understanding of what is heard to highly developed writing and speaking skills. For example, a person who has grown up in the United States in a household where grandparents speak a language other than English may be able to understand them, but be unable to respond in that language and possess virtually no literacy skills. Such heritage speakers possess a rich cultural tradition but need to develop their language skills. Other heritage speakers may be quite bilingual, somewhere along a continuum ranging from informal usage only to application in a wide variety of professional and academic settings.

Heritage speakers might be recruited through scholarships from community or heritage organizations, because these groups have a direct interest in maintaining their language and culture. Some state organizations serving the needs of recent immigrants, for example, have provided scholarships and encouragement for young adults to enter teacher training programs in order to obtain employment as bilingual teaching aides, bilingual classroom teachers, or language teachers to mainly native English speakers. Such efforts provide incentives for

heritage students to serve the language needs of the local language community by becoming educators, assisting other heritage speakers and students. This is one way to help provide a supply of teachers for the less commonly taught languages in schools, such as Japanese, Italian, Hebrew, Arabic, and American Sign Language. Heritage speakers possess language skills and cultural knowledge upon which they can build as they prepare to teach the language of their heritage. With such prior knowledge and skill, these future teachers begin at a more advanced level in their language training and can thus concentrate more quickly on the specific strategies needed to teach languages. Such a valuable resource must be tapped to increase the number of U.S. schools offering Arabic, Chinese, Indonesian, and other non-European languages.

4. In the current era of statewide accountability, how can my district design a world language program with appropriate allocations of time?

Time is the single greatest factor affecting the development of students' language proficiency. Experience in elementary and middle school programs shows that instruction of less than three sessions per week is not very efficient in developing any degree of proficiency. Over time, the lack of results from such programs leads to their demise. Many well-meaning world language programs focus only on once-a-week instruction beginning in kindergarten. The grade to begin a world language program is the earliest grade possible for sustaining, from that point forward, a frequency of three or more sessions per week.

The same holds true in middle school grades. To develop language proficiency, a sampling of several languages provides a minimal start. Allowing students to begin a language of their choice in middle school, if not sooner, and continue to study that language continuously through high school graduation is a more defensible program option. Remembering that world language instruction provides a strong development of reading, listening, writing, and speaking skills, school administrators can confidently offer and schedule more frequent and continuous world language classes. Scheduling more class time for reading or language arts is not the only way to prepare students for state testing in those areas. Providing a program for learning another language strongly supports student achievement in reading and language arts.

The North Carolina Department of Public Instruction (2003) has published a resource that explores how elementary schools can bring balance to the curriculum, providing sufficient frequency and length of instruction to provide all students a basic education that includes world languages. *The Balanced Curriculum* is available at the North Carolina Department of Public Instruction's Web site (www.ncpublicschools.org/curriculum).

Content-related instruction is essential for teaching world languages in elementary grades. The school day is already packed with school subjects. The important guiding principle for world language program design is not to cut something out of the curriculum in order to bring in languages, but rather to identify specific content (curriculum units, concepts, knowledge, and skills) that can appropriately be taught through the target language. At times, the language teacher might preteach elements of a unit. Prior to a classroom teacher beginning a unit on the solar system, for example, the language teacher might cover such content as the names of the planets, their order from the sun, the distances between them, relative climate differences, circumferences and diameters of the planets, and how long their days and years are. All of these facts can be learned with simple language involving descriptive phrases and numbers, the kind of language at the command of even the most beginning language students.

At times, the language teacher might coteach a unit with the classroom teacher. For example, when a 4th grade Wisconsin teacher introduces a unit on that state, the language teacher might take students on the path of the *voyageurs*, singing French traveling songs as she traces the journey of the explorers and early fur traders who traveled through the state, naming geographical places with French names and greeting the Native Americans. Through the language instruction, students come to a deeper understanding of the French experience and heritage in the state, supporting but not duplicating what the classroom teacher is doing in English.

Another option for the language teacher is reteaching or practicing what the classroom teacher has taught. A prime example would be graphing techniques and applications. Once the classroom teacher has given an overview of the basic approaches to graphing, the language teacher can be in charge of practicing graphing during the rest of the year. Graphing is a natural way to learn and discuss vocabulary, as students physically manipulate figures to classify objects or adjectives into various categories. Graphing could be practiced to discuss different housing in the community, the heritage of families in the school, characteristics that different animals have in common, and endless other possibilities.

Middle schools might also consider such a content-related approach. Some middle schools have placed a world language teacher on each interdisciplinary team. The language instruction then can be related more easily to the thematic units of the team. The language teacher prepares units that develop students' language proficiency and also build up their knowledge of the topics.

Figure 11 shows options that have been proposed or implemented in middle schools in

Wisconsin. The models demonstrate some creative applications of these principles in scheduling middle school courses that include sufficient amounts of time for the development of proficiency in a world language.

5. Why is it important to demonstrate student proficiency in elementary grades, middle school, and senior high programs?

The public demand for results is closely related to the question of the appropriate allocation of time for an effective program. Very few states require any type of assessment of world languages. State education agencies may provide assistance with the design of world language assessment or sample assessments, but not the type of assessment that currently directs program design in the tested areas of English language arts and reading, social studies, science, and mathematics. Without state assessment of students' skills and knowledge in languages other than English, local districts need to prove the value of their

programs with appropriate evidence. Such evidence should capture language performances in terms that the public expects and accepts, that is, evidence showing real-world application of the language. Assessments should provide evidence of how well students hold conversations with native speakers, understand the gist of written and spoken messages, and present information in ways that are linguistically and culturally appropriate.

Districts that are consciously addressing these issues of assessment will be ready to respond when different groups ask for a justification of their program(s). This question will come from a variety of sources: the middle school language teacher will ask it of the elementary language teacher; the senior high language teacher will ask it of the middle school teacher; university faculty in charge of language placement will ask for such evidence from the senior high staff; school boards will ask administrators to show how effective the program is; the public will want evidence of what students are actually learning as a result of their investment in the

Figure 11 Middle School Schedule Options	
Varying Choices (Eight-Period Day)	
Grade 7	**Grade 8**
Yearlong Courses (five periods per day)	
English	English
Social Studies	Social Studies
Math	Math
Science	Science
P.E. / Health	P.E. / Health
Single-Semester Courses (three periods per day)	
(One semester each; all required)	*(Choose any combination to total six semesters)*
Art / Music	Music / Art / Business Ed
Tech Ed / Family & Consumer Ed	Tech Ed / Family & Consumer Ed
Computers / World Language	World Language (for two semesters)

Figure 11 (_continued_)	
Middle School Schedule Options	
Two Interdisciplinary Teams (Nine-Period Day)*	
Humanities Block (six periods per day)	
English	Daily
Social Studies	Daily
World Language	Daily
P.E. / Family & Consumer Ed	Alternating Days
Art / Music	Alternating Days
Resource / Study / Advisor-Advisee	Daily
Technology Block (three periods per day)	
Science	Daily
Mathematics	Daily
Tech Ed / Computer Ed	Alternating Days
*Teachers spend two-thirds of the day involved in teaching and classroom assignments; the remaining one-third of the day is split between team planning and individual planning.	
New Team Clusters (Eight-Period Day, includes Lunch)	
Group A: Two-and-a-Half Periods	
English	
Social Studies	Group A includes instruction in reading through the three content areas (not as a separate course).
World Languages	
Group B: Two-and-a-Half Periods	
Mathematics	
Science	Group B includes instruction in computer technology through the three content areas (not as a separate course).
Tech Ed	
Group C: One-and-a-Half Periods	
Family and Consumer Ed	
Health	Group C determines how to use the one-and-a-half periods each day (could be a single subject on one day, a half-period for each subject on another day, or any combination of two or three subjects, as needed).
Physical Education	
Group D: One Period	
Art	
Music	Group D determines how to use the daily period (could be a single subject on a given day, or the period could be divided to cover both subjects, as needed).
Lunch: One-Half Period	
Students eat in advisor/advisee groups or in homeroom groups, as needed.	

Figure 11 (*continued*)
Middle School Schedule Options

Small-School Variation (Seven-Period Day, plus Lunch)

Grade 6	Grade 7	Grade 8
Yearlong Courses (four periods per day)		
English	English	English
Social Studies	Social Studies	Social Studies
Mathematics	Mathematics	Mathematics
Science	Science	Science
Various Courses (three periods per day)		
Electives: World Language / Study Skills	**Electives:** World Language / Study Skills	**Electives:** World Language / Study Skills
Alternate Days: Music / P.E. & Health	**Alternate Days:** Music / P.E. & Health	**Alternate Days:** Music / P.E. & Health
12 Weeks Each: Computer Skills / Tech Ed / Art	**12 Weeks Each:** Family & Consumer Ed / Tech Ed / Art	**12 Weeks Each:** Family & Consumer Ed / Tech Ed / Art
Lunch		
Students get 20 minutes to eat and 40 minutes for Band, Orchestra, or Choir (for those students electing such music offerings).		

Options Within Options (Eight-Period Day)

Grade 6	Grade 7	Grade 8*	
Yearlong Courses (six periods per day)			
English	English	English	
Social Studies	Social Studies	Social Studies	
Mathematics	Mathematics	Mathematics	
Science	Science	Science	
Reading	Literature	Electives as for grades 6 and 7	
P.E. / Health (EOD)**	P.E. / Health (EOD)	P.E. / Health (EOD)	
Option Courses (two periods per day)			
Electives: Study Hall Band Chorus Photography	**Electives:** Study Hall Band Chorus Photography	**Option A:** World Languages (all year)	**Option B:** Literature (one semester) Careers (one semester)

Figure 11 (continued) Middle School Schedule Options			
Option Courses (two periods per day) (continued)			

Art
  (one quarter)
Music
  (one quarter)
Study Skills
  (one quarter)
World Languages
  (one quarter)
	World Languages
	  (one semester)
	Computers
	  (one quarter)
	Art
	  (one quarter)
		Option A:
		Music
		  (one quarter)
		Computers
		  (one quarter)
		Careers
		  (one semester)
			Option B:
			Music
			  (one quarter)
			Computers
			  (one quarter)
			Art
			  (one quarter)
			Choose one of the three
			(Music, Computers, Art) for
			an additional quarter.

*Students in Grade 8 select Option A or Option B (cannot select one period from Option A and one period from Option B); this covers courses for two periods of the day. **EOD = Every Other Day / All Year			

Source: Adapted from material collected in Wisconsin schools by Paul Sandrock, 2000. Unpublished data. Adapted with permission.

program; and parents and students will need proof that students have learned something of practical value. By providing assessment that fits these demands—not tests on grammar and vocabulary but assessment showing real language applications—teachers and administrators will help all of these groups understand the true goals of the program. Assessment of this nature makes a very positive statement about the skills being developed in students, and measurable proof of achievement will help language programs survive in tough budget times.

6. Where can I find adequate resources to implement an effective program?

Instructional Materials

Thanks to technology, the wealth of powerful and affordable resources now available to teachers of world languages is almost immeasurable. This statement is not meant to imply that traditional instructional materials are ineffective; technology merely opens the door to myriad possibilities. What has been said about reform-based/standards-based learning and teaching in this chapter supports the use of multiple resources for language instruction and assessment. It also provides food for thought in terms of the need to reevaluate the use of a textbook as the sole or primary resource in a world language program. For example, the use of Internet materials minimizes the costs incurred in purchasing textbooks for all students and is a pedagogically sound alternative. Online technologies enable students to access up-to-date and up-to-the-minute authentic cultural materials and realia. The use of e-mail, electronic conferencing, and online performance assessments are only a few of the many instructional tools available that provide a means for real-life communication. Audio and video segments that illustrate a wide variety of speakers of a given language provide access to many speaking styles, voices, and accents while providing a realistic look at the target culture that is not possible through conventional means. (For further examples of technology use in language instruction, see Designing and Implementing Flexible World Language Programs in Major Trends and Issues).

In addition, by the very nature of the profession, world language teachers are fortunate in being able to obtain instructional materials through various embassies and consulates that represent the language and culture being taught, heritage-language community resources, and international exchanges and trips. Teachers also have access to resources available through other means, such as language- and nonlanguage-specific organizations, through listservers, or at workshops and conferences, for example.

Curriculum Development

The New Visions in Action (NVIA) Project, a national grant-funded initiative, seeks to identify and implement the actions necessary to revamp the language education system so that it can more effectively achieve the important goal of language proficiency for all students. The goal of the Curriculum, Instruction, Assessment, and Articulation Task Force of the NVIA Project is to produce online and paper documents that synthesize information for guiding and informing local decision making in the areas of curriculum, instruction, assessment, and articulation. The information obtained from this project is available online at no cost to educators at www.educ.iastate.edu/newvisions and represents a reliable source to inform work done in these areas.

Information on curriculum development and related topics also is available on most of the 50 states' Web sites, as well as through the National Foreign Language Resource Centers, funded by grants from the U.S. Department of Education. Their mission is to facilitate the improvement of the teaching and learning of foreign languages in the United States. Currently, 14 centers exist nationwide, each having a different focus (see the Curriculum Resources section). For example, the National K–12 Foreign Language Resource Center at Iowa State University focuses solely on the improvement of student learning of foreign languages at the elementary and secondary school levels. The center conducts research, develops publications, and holds summer institutes for teachers that revolve around the themes of curriculum development, innovative technology, performance assessment, action research, foreign language student standards, and professional collaboration. Past projects include the creation of a guide to assist teachers in aligning their present foreign language curriculum with the national standards for student learning. The document enables teachers to identify what aspects of their current curriculum fit with the standards and how these can be extended and adapted to address the new dimensions of the standards. The center also has created thematic units to assist with content-related teaching at the elementary level.

7. How do I apply the vision of standards-based language instruction in my classroom? Where do I begin?

One way to begin to transition your practice from a more traditional textbook approach to a more standards-driven approach to language learning is by doing an honest self-assessment of your teaching. Figure 12 provides an excellent starting point and also may be used for the purposes of teacher observation by supervisors. After completing the self-assessment, you may wish to consider (1) new ideas or questions this chapter of the handbook raised for you and (2) actions you intend to take in response.

The following questions and prompts are designed to be considered in discussions about your district language program with your colleagues or staff. They were compiled by New Jersey supervisors of world languages for the purpose of evaluation and may be duplicated for educational purposes. After discussing the questions, you and your colleagues or staff may wish to consider (1) new ideas or questions raised by this chapter of the *Handbook* and (2) actions you intend to take in response.

Figure 12 Standards-Driven Instruction and Assessment Rubric			
The Teacher	**Yes (3)**	**Sometimes (2)**	**No (1)**
1 Do you use the language easily and most of the time?			
2 Do you supplement language use with visual cues to enhance comprehension?			
3 Do you move around the classroom and use proximity to students to encourage participation and limit disciplinary problems?			
4 Do you involve all students in the class?			
5 Do you change activities frequently enough to encourage use of a variety of learning modes and to reinforce a variety of content and skills?			
6 Does your instruction include elements that reinforce learning through visual, auditory, and kinesthetic cues?			
7 Are students guided to use all levels of thinking skills (e.g., they repeat, recognize, and recall as well as apply, create, and predict)?			
8 Is assessment ongoing? Are students assessed formally and informally on how well they meet the objectives of the lesson?			
The Students			
1 Do the students communicate with the teacher and with each other in the target language?			
2 Is there more student activity than teacher activity?			
3 Do students take risks as language learners?			
4 Do students use the text as a resource rather than the main focus of instruction?			
5 Do students demonstrate the ability to use the language for communication (i.e., do they do more than conjugate verbs, write vocabulary words, or recite rules)?			
The Standards			
1 Communication—Are communicative modes (interpersonal, interpretive, presentational) addressed in the lesson?			
2 Culture—Is there evidence of cultural elements that reinforce the communicative elements being introduced?			
3 Connections—Is there evidence of integration of content from other disciplines?			
4 Comparisons—Are students asked to make comparisons of language or culture?			
5 Communities—Are students using the language outside of the classroom?			

Source: From Standards-Driven Instruction and Assessment Rubric developed by the Supervisors of World Languages Model Program Initiative, 2002. Reprinted with permission.

1. Are ongoing professional development opportunities available for the world language staff, both in-district and out-of-district?

2. Do world language teachers have common planning time available for curriculum development? Is planning time provided to foster curriculum integration with other content area teachers?

3. Describe the assessment philosophy and types of assessments used in the world languages program.

4. How does the school district provide for both vertical and horizontal articulation among schools in the district?

5. How are students grouped for world language instruction? How are needs met for the special education population? For heritage-language learners?

6. How are world languages scheduled in the school day at the elementary and middle school levels?

7. To what degree do the school administration, the board of education, and the community support the world language program?

8. Describe any areas that need improvement in your program.

9. Identify the strongest components of your program.

WORKS CITED

Gardner, H. (1983). *Frames of mind: The theory of multiple intelligences*. New York: Basic.

Gifford, C. (2004, April 14). *Spanish for the professions: Getting the job done*. Presentation given at the Northeast Conference on the Teaching of Foreign Languages.

Nebraska Department of Education. (1996). *Nebraska K–12 foreign language frameworks*. Lincoln, NE: Author.

New Jersey Department of Education. (1999). *New Jersey world languages curriculum framework*. Trenton, NJ: Author.

New Jersey Department of Education. (2004). *Academic and professional standards: World languages*. Retrieved April 26, 2005, from www.state.nj.us/njded/aps/cccs/wl/regs.htm

North Carolina Department of Public Instruction. (2003, November). *The balanced curriculum: A guiding document for scheduling and implementation of the NC standard course of study at the elementary level*. Retrieved April 26, 2005, from http://www.ncpublicschools.org/curriculum

Samaniego, F., & Pino, C. (2000). Frequently asked questions about SNS programs. In N. Anderson (Ed.), *AATSP professional development series handbook for teachers K–16, volume I: Spanish for native speakers* (pp. 29–64). Fort Worth, TX: Harcourt College.

Sandrock, P. (2000). [Middle school schedules]. Unpublished raw data.

Supervisors of World Languages Model Program Initiative. (2002). [Standards-driven instruction and assessment rubric]. Unpublished material.

Valdes, G. (2001). Heritage language students: Profiles and possibilities. In J. K. Peyton, D. Ranard, & S. McGinnis (Eds.), *Heritage languages in America: Preserving a national resource* (pp. 37–77). McHenry, IL: Delta Systems; and Washington, DC: Center for Applied Linguistics.

IV. CURRICULUM RESOURCES

ORGANIZATIONS

Numerous organizations promote the principles and activities supportive of effective world language instructional programs and curriculum development as described in this ASCD *Handbook* chapter. The leading organization coordinating these efforts is the American Council on the Teaching of Foreign Languages (ACTFL), whose assembly of delegate organizations includes most of the language-specific, national, and regional organizations included here. These listed organizations provide leadership for the teaching and learning of languages from specific perspectives: local school districts, institutions of higher education, state education agencies, heritage-language learners, and early language learning.

American Council on the Teaching of Foreign Languages (ACTFL)

700 S. Washington St., Suite 210
Alexandria, VA 22314
www.actfl.org

ACTFL's mission is to provide vision, leadership, and support for quality teaching and learning of languages. From the development of proficiency guidelines to a leadership role in the creation of national and language-specific standards, from representation for languages in cross-curricular initiatives to the implementation of innovations in teacher training, ACTFL focuses on issues that are critical to the growth of the profession and the individual teacher.

The links provided through the ACTFL Web site are current and comprehensive in the following areas:

- Business Partners

- Cultural Information

- Funding Agencies

- Information Resources

- National Language Organizations

- National Language Resource Centers

- Regional Language Associations

- Search Engines

- State Departments of Education

- State Language Associations

- State Language Frameworks

- Year of Languages

National Association of District Supervisors of Foreign Languages (NADSFL)

http://nadsfl.org/index

NADSFL gives support to department heads and district-level coordinators of world language programs.

National Council of State Supervisors for Languages (NCSSFL)

www.ncssfl.org

NCSSFL provides annual state-by-state reports on world language legislation, policies, and initiatives; position papers on critical issues affecting language learning; links to state world language standards and frameworks; and contact information for state supervisors.

Alliance for the Advancement of Heritage Languages

www.cal.org/heritage

This alliance promotes the conservation and development of the heritage-language resources of the United States in order to produce citizens who can function professionally in English and other languages.

Language-Specific Organizations

The following national language-specific organizations provide support to language teachers through professional development, advocacy, and resources for teaching. These organizations represent the languages more commonly taught in schools in the United States.

American Association of Teachers of Arabic
www.wm.edu/aata

American Association of Teachers of French
www.frenchteachers.org

American Association of Teachers of German
www.aatg.org

American Association of Teachers of Italian
www.aati-online.org

American Association of Teachers of Slavic and East European Languages
http://aatseel.org

American Association of Teachers of Spanish and Portuguese
http://aatsp.org

American Classical League (for teachers of Latin and Greek)
www.aclclassics.org

American Council of Teachers of Russian
www.americancouncils.org

Chinese Language Teachers Association
http://clta.osu.edu

National Council of Japanese Language Teachers (NCJLT)
www.ncjlt.org

Regional Language Organizations

These five organizations provide professional development at a regional level and work with and through state organizations of language educators.

Central States Conference on the Teaching of Foreign Languages
www.centralstates.cc

Northeast Conference on the Teaching of Foreign Languages
http://omega.dickinson.edu/nectfl

Pacific Northwest Council for Languages
http://babel.uoregon.edu/pncfl

Southern Conference on Language Teaching
www.valdosta.edu/scolt

Southwest Conference on Language Teaching
www.swcolt.org

NATIONAL LANGUAGE RESOURCE CENTERS

Foreign Language Resource Centers Home Page
http://nflrc.msu.edu

The U.S. Department of Education has awarded grants to a small number of institutions for the purpose of establishing, strengthening, and operating national foreign language resource and training centers to improve the teaching and learning of foreign languages. Currently, 14 Title VI Language Resource Centers exist nationwide, each with a particular area of concentration.

Center for Advanced Language Proficiency Education and Research (CALPER)
Pennsylvania State University
http://calper.la.psu.edu

CALPER focuses on improving the environment of advanced-level foreign language teaching, learning, and assessment. It conducts research, develops teaching and learning materials, and provides educational opportunities for language professionals.

Center for Advanced Research on Language Acquisition (CARLA)

University of Minnesota

www.carla.umn.edu

CARLA studies multilingualism and multiculturalism to develop knowledge of second-language acquisition and to advance the quality of second-language teaching, learning, and assessment. CARLA offers a number of resources to language teachers, including a battery of second-language proficiency assessments and a series of working papers.

Center for Applied Second Language Studies (CASLS)

University of Oregon

http://casls.uoregon.edu/home.php

CASLS promotes international literacy by supporting communities of educators and by partnering with those communities to develop a comprehensive system of proficiency-based tools for lifelong language learning and teaching. CASLS works with K–16 teams of teachers to develop content-based thematic units, including authentic materials and performance assessments.

Center for Language Education and Research (CLEAR)

Michigan State University

http://clear.msu.edu

CLEAR develops materials and conducts research for foreign language teaching and learning and provides professional development opportunities for educators in the field. Projects relate to classroom practice and address commonalities across languages.

Center for Languages of the Central Asian Region (CELCAR)

Indiana University

www.indiana.edu/~celcar

CELCAR seeks to enhance U.S. national capacity for teaching and learning the languages and cultures of Central Asia and surrounding regions.

Language Acquisition Resource Center (LARC)

San Diego State University

http://larcnet.sdsu.edu

LARC develops and supports the teaching and learning of foreign languages in the United States through research, technology, and publications. Particular attention is paid to less commonly taught languages, cross-cultural issues, language skills assessment, and teacher training.

National African Language Resource Center (NALRC)

University of Wisconsin

http://african.lss.wisc.edu/nalrc

NALRC serves the entire community of African language educators and learners in the United States by sponsoring a wide range of educational and professional activities designed to improve the accessibility and quality of African language instruction in the United States.

National Capital Language Resource Center (NCLRC)

Georgetown University Center for Applied Linguistics

www.nclrc.org

NCLRC serves as a resource to improve the teaching and learning of foreign languages by providing material resources and professional services that derive from its activities and projects. It publishes a monthly electronic newsletter and online resources for the teaching of culture in a variety of languages.

National East Asian Languages Resource Center (NEALRC)
Ohio State University
www.flc.osu.edu

NEALRC serves the needs of learners and teachers of East Asian languages through initiatives designed to increase learners' abilities to master advanced levels of language and cultural competence.

National Foreign Language Resource Center (NFLRC)
University of Hawaii at Manoa
www.nflrc.hawaii.edu

NFLRC undertakes projects that focus primarily on the less commonly taught languages of East Asia, Southeast Asia, and the Pacific. Many of its projects have implications for the teaching and learning of all languages and have the overriding goal of developing prototypes that can be applied broadly as resources to improve foreign language education nationally.

National K–12 Foreign Language Resource Center (NFLRC)
Iowa State University
www.educ.iastate.edu/nflrc

NFLRC's mission is to improve student learning of foreign languages in kindergarten through 12th grade throughout the United States. NFLRC is well known nationally for its excellent summer institutes, publications, and research.

National Middle East Language Resource Center (NMELRC)
Brigham Young University
http://nmelrc.byu.edu

NMELRC coordinates efforts aimed at increasing and improving opportunities for learning the languages of the Middle East. The center undertakes and supports teacher training, materials development, testing and assessment, integration of pedagogy and technology, study abroad, and K–12 programs.

Slavic and East European Language Resource Center (SEELRC)
Duke University & University of North Carolina
http://seelrc.org

SEELRC's goal is to improve the national capacity to teach and learn Slavic and East European languages by developing teaching and assessment materials and by supporting research and other activities, including undergraduate and graduate education and exchange programs, conferences, seminars, and public outreach programs.

South Asia Language Resource Center (SALRC)
University of Chicago
http://salrc.uchicago.edu

SALRC is the umbrella organization under which less commonly taught languages are advanced through a coordinated program to improve the national infrastructure for language teaching and learning. It creates and disseminates new resources for teaching and research with other institutions having overlapping language interests, most notably those for the Middle East and Central Asia.

POLICY AND ADVOCACY
International Ed.org Web Site
www.internationaled.org

International Ed.org is a Web site that provides curricular resources, research, and information on initiatives that support international studies in schools. It provides resources that support efforts to increase knowledge about other world regions and cultures, other languages, and international issues. The site contains links to international projects and activities in the United States and information on new programs related to critical-need languages.

Joint National Committee for Languages and the National Council for Languages and International Studies (JNCL-NCLIS)
www.languagepolicy.org

JNCL is a coalition of more than 60 organizations that encompasses virtually all areas of the language profession. It functions as a point of reference for the identification of national needs and the planning of national language policies. NCLIS is a registered lobbying organization and serves as the "action arm" for the language and international education communities. The Web site contains valuable links and information on advocacy and federal and state legislation affecting language programs.

Minnesota New Visions: Languages for Life
www.mctlc.org/newvisions/prresources.html

This Web site includes links and information about a variety of resources including brochures and videos that promote language learning; articles and reports that give background information and overviews on language learning; databases of information on language learning; advocacy resources; and other resources for language teachers.

2004 National Language Conference
www.nlconference.org

This site contains papers presented by experts in government, business, and education that offer examples of international best practices, models for K–16 language education, and state and national language policies.

New Visions in Action: Foreign Language Education
www.educ.iastate.edu/newvisions

New Visions in Action has coordinated the work of numerous world language organizations to create common purpose and effective efforts focusing on curriculum, instruction, articulation and assessment, second-language research, and teacher recruitment and retention. The project's Web site offers checklists with criteria of excellence to guide program planners and implementers.

Office of English Language Acquisition, Language Enhancement, and Academic Achievement for Limited English Proficient Students
www.ed.gov/about/offices/list/oela

OELA's primary goal is to identify major issues affecting the education of English language learners. OELA also is the program office for foreign language instruction and administers the Foreign Language Assistance Program (FLAP). This program makes available grants to pay for the federal share of the cost of innovative model programs providing for the establishment, improvement, or expansion of foreign language study for elementary and secondary school students.

The Alliance for Language Learning
www.allianceforlanguagelearning.org

The Alliance for Language Learning is an advocacy group made up of business, higher education, and community leaders in North Carolina that sponsors North Carolina's K–12 articulation program, VISION 2010. The Web site contains examples of models of articulation and other resources.

The European Centre for Modern Languages

www.ecml.at

This site contains information on the implementation of language policies and promotion of innovative approaches to the learning and teaching of modern languages.

Year of Languages

www.yearoflanguages.org

Year of Languages is a national advocacy effort designed to create public interest in and support for learning languages. Activities during the year 2005 will celebrate and highlight language diversity and opportunities to learn languages from elementary grades through adulthood. These activities begin a decade-long emphasis, through 2015, on the goal of realizing the vision of languages for all.

EARLY LANGUAGE LEARNING
Ñandu

www.cal.org/earlylang/nandu.htm

Ñandu is a listserver for school district personnel, superintendents, teachers, college and university teacher educators, and parents. It is sponsored by the Improving Foreign Language Instruction Project of the Northeast and Islands Regional Educational Laboratory at Brown University (LAB) and is funded by the U.S. Department of Education.

Ñandutí

www.cal.org/earlylang

Available through the same site as Ñandu, Ñandutí is a resource on foreign language learning in grades K–8 that offers information on the bene-

fits of early foreign language learning, advocacy, how to start a K–8 program, integrating content into language instruction, using technology, and assessing student progress. It also contains a national directory of early language learning programs.

Foreign Language Study and the Brain

http://ivcusers.ed.uidaho.edu/tkennedy/flbrain/

This site provides information on the relationship of brain research to effective foreign language instruction at the elementary level and after puberty.

National Network for Early Language Learning (NNELL)

www.nnell.org

NNELL is an organization for educators involved in teaching foreign languages to children. NNELL provides leadership, support, and service to those committed to early language learning and coordinates efforts to make language learning in programs of excellence a reality for all children. NNELL publishes the journal *Learning Languages* twice a year. The Members Only section of the Web site contains a detailed Members Directory, a subsection on advocacy, a message board, access to classroom activities and lesson plans, and a complete subsection on building an early language-learning program.

SEEDS (Support for Elementary Educators Through Distance Education in Spanish)

http://seeds.coedu.usf.edu/index2.htm

This Title VI federal grant project is designed to develop three distance-education modules, available on CD-ROM and through the Web. The modules are (1) Spanish Enhancement, (2) Teaching Spanish as a Foreign Language, and (3) Internationalizing the Elementary Curriculum.

The Balanced Curriculum: A Guiding Document for Scheduling and Implementation of the NC Standard Course of Study at the Elementary Level

www.ncpublicschools.org/curriculum

This document (available in PDF format only—requires Adobe Acrobat) from the North Carolina Department of Public Instruction focuses on the importance and value of a well-rounded education that includes learning languages. The document provides guiding principles and recommendations, sample scenarios and schedules, and resources to implement such a curriculum.

The GLOBE Program

www.globe.gov

The GLOBE Program is a worldwide, hands-on, primary and secondary school-based education and science program that can be used to integrate science concepts into the world language classroom. The Web site links to a number of sites with information, activities, and opportunities related to the goals of the GLOBE Program.

LANGUAGE TEACHING RESOURCES

Bibliography of Modern Foreign Languages and Special Education Needs

www.specialeducationalneeds.com

This 2004 international bibliography contains valuable resources on special-needs students in second-language programs at all levels of instruction. Topics include students with cognitive and learning needs, emotional and behavioral needs, and sensory and physical needs. (Note: The URL provided leads to the professional page of the bibliography's author, David R. Wilson. Scroll down the page to select the link titled "Bibliographies of special educational needs in school subject teaching," located under "Word Documents." Accessing this page leads to a list of subject area links, including

"Modern Foreign Languages," which opens a Microsoft Word file.)

Center for Applied Linguistics

www.cal.org

The center creates publications, conducts research, gathers articles and information, and develops projects to further the teaching and learning of languages in a variety of settings: language courses for English speakers; K–12 immersion programs, including dual-language immersion and content-based immersion; bilingual education; and teaching English as a second language.

CoBaLTT (Content-Based Language Teaching with Technology)

www.carla.umn.edu/cobaltt

This Web site features lesson plans and units developed by teachers during yearlong professional development projects on standards- and content-based instruction and curriculum.

Computer Assisted Language Instruction Consortium (CALICO)

www.calico.org

This professional organization focuses on both education and technology, with an emphasis on language teaching and learning. The Web site features a clearinghouse of information on computer-assisted language learning.

Education Resources Information Center (ERIC)

www.eric.ed.gov

ERIC's a digital library consists primarily of electronic bibliographic records describing journal and nonjournal literature on languages and linguistics as well as other topics selected by ERIC from 1966–2003. The site provides extensive search functionality by topic as well as an electronic question-and-answer service, Ask ERIC.

Foreign Language Teaching Forum (FL Teach)
www.cortland.edu/flteach

This listserver connects more than 4,000 educators, mainly in the United States but also in 60 other countries, to discuss issues in teaching languages at all levels, including school/college articulation, training of student teachers, classroom activities, curriculum, and syllabus design. Participants—including preservice teacher candidates, methods professors, new and veteran teachers, and administrators—also have access to an extensive archive.

Foreign Embassies of Washington, D.C.
www.embassy.org/embassies

The Foreign Embassies of Washington, D.C., often develop classroom resources and offer study opportunities for language teachers through their education offices. This site maintains updated listings of Web sites for embassies of foreign governments in the United States.

Fulbright Teacher and Administrator Exchange Program
www.fulbrightexchanges.org

This organization coordinates programs to bring educators from other countries for short- and long-term study seminars in the United States and for U.S. educators to learn abroad through focused study projects.

International Association for Language Learning Technology
http://iall.net

This association provides leadership in the development, integration, evaluation, and management of instructional technology for the teaching and learning of languages, literature, and culture.

International Education and Resource Network (iEARN)
http://iearn.org

This online, project-based network of schools links students and teachers from more than 100 countries around the world.

The Virtual Assessment Center
www.carla.umn.edu/assessment/vac

This professional development module guides teachers through the creation of performance assessments for use in their classrooms.

V. ASCD RESOURCES

For more information about these and other ASCD resources, contact the ASCD Service Center at 1-800-933-2723 or 1-703-578-9600 between 8:00 a.m. and 5:00 p.m. Monday through Friday, eastern time, or visit ASCD's Online Store at http://shop.ascd.org.

BOOK

Meeting the Needs of Second Language Learners: An Educator's Guide
By Judith Lessow-Hurley

In a multilingual society, confusion and controversy sometimes surround the teaching of students. This book offers readers sound principles and advice for second-language program development.

Among the topics Lessow-Hurley examines in her consideration of the challenges and triumphs of helping second-language learners succeed are

- Why understanding the differences between additive and subtractive bilingualism is critical.

- Qualities to look for in a good bilingual teacher.

- How primary language instruction supports academic success.

- Why the term "immersion" is commonly misunderstood and misused.

- Commonly used bilingual program models.

Stock #102043
Price: $13.95 for ASCD members
         $16.95 for nonmembers

ASCD NETWORKS

The following ASCD networks may be of interest to educators seeking contacts and additional information about world language instruction and issues.

Global Education

- Develops and sustains communication on global and multicultural perspectives and initiatives.

- Provides programming and resources for global education and plays an advocacy role in support of the same.

- Provides a vehicle for mutual assistance, allowing members to share information about models and best practices, challenges, and solutions.

Network Facilitators
Anne Baker
Phone: 1-202-293-7728, ext. 12
Fax: 1-202-293-7554
E-mail: globaled@rpcv.org

Doug Schermer
Phone: 1-319-256-6002
E-mail: dschermer@farmtel.net

Hispanic/Latino-American Critical Issues
Web site: www.fascd.org/hcin/home.asp

- Is committed to enhancing the academic achievement of Hispanic/Latino-American youth.

- Serves as a forum on contemporary and relevant issues as related to the education of Hispanic/Latino-American youth.

- Strives to narrow the achievement gap and increase input of Hispanic/Latino-American educators on relevant educational issues.

Network Facilitators
Eduardo Rivas
Phone: 1-305-995-2561
Fax: 1-305-995-1520
E-mail: erivas@dadeschools.net

Carlos Viera
Phone: 1-305-995-7597
Fax: 1-305-995-4189
E-mail: cviera@dadeschools.net

Language Varieties (Pidgins, Creoles, & Other Stigmatized Varieties)
Web site: www.une.edu.au/langnet

■ Provides a forum for dialogue about variant-language issues in education.

■ Provides a network of information about pidgins, Creoles, and other stigmatized varieties, thereby increasing understanding of variant-language issues.

Network Facilitator
Ermile Hargrove
Phone: 1-808-247-9511
E-mail: Ekhargrove@aol.com

PROFESSIONAL INQUIRY KIT

Educating Linguistically and Culturally Diverse Students: An ASCD Professional Inquiry Kit
By Belinda Williams

Use of this kit in small groups offers participants the opportunity to learn and apply new ideas on educating linguistically and culturally diverse students. Participants explore common theories, research, and practice important to educating diverse student populations, including techniques for ESL learners.

The first folder in the eight-folder series provides teachers with a rationale for and clear instructions on forming a successful study group. The remaining folders are titled

■ Why Educating Diverse Student Populations Requires Leadership for Change

■ Culture and Learning: Guidelines for Considering Culture and Its Influence on Teaching and Learning

■ Appropriate Instruction for English Language Learners: Emphasis on Oral Interaction

■ What Standards-Based Learning Means for Culturally and Linguistically Diverse Schools

■ Initiating and Sustaining Meaningful School-wide Reforms

■ Professional Development: Strategies for Improved Achievement

■ Extending Your Learning

Stock #998060
Price: $189 for ASCD members
          $220 for nonmembers

VIDEOTAPES

A Visit to a Classroom of English Language Learners

Spend a day at a world-renowned bilingual school—the first dual-language public school in the United States—to get an up-close-and-personal tour of the programs and practices proven successful for students who are learning English.

Following a 2nd grade class through their language arts, science, math, and social studies lessons, this video showcases the best practices that teachers use to address the needs of English language learners, including

■ Immersion in a content-based language approach where students learn academic content, vocabulary, and language patterns simultaneously.

■ Second-language teaching strategies, such as visuals, total physical response, verbal interaction, learning buddies, read aloud, and the use of repetition.

Use this video for professional development meetings, study groups, teams, and individual teacher observation to demonstrate the action steps for developing dual-language instruction.

Stock #404447

Price: $145 for ASCD members
$170 for nonmembers

Maximizing Learning for English Language Learners (Tapes 1–3)—Entire Series

This professional development tool helps teachers and administrators address the needs of English language learners (ELL) through solid techniques. Use the three videotapes and accompanying facilitator's guide to create workshops and presentations that inform teachers and other audiences of proven approaches.

Stock #403326

Price: $440 for ASCD members
$540 for nonmembers

WEB SITE

For a complete listing of ASCD books in different languages, visit us on the Web at www.ascd.org /ascdworld and follow the link to ASCD Books in Translation.

ASCD ARTICLES

The articles reprinted in the following pages address issues related to this *Curriculum Handbook* chapter on world languages. The articles are not intended to express ASCD's position on the topics in question; they are included to help curriculum planners better understand the issues and practices relating to world language study.

"How Global Is the Curriculum?"
By Andrew F. Smith
Educational Leadership, October 2002

"Two-Way Immersion: A Key to Global Awareness"
By Elizabeth R. Howard
Educational Leadership, October 2002

"Language Learning: A Worldwide Perspective"
By Donna Christian, Ingrid U. Pufahl, and Nancy C. Rhodes
Educational Leadership, December 2004/January 2005

"U.S. World Language Program Models"
By Audrey L. Heining-Boynton
Educational Leadership, December 2004/January 2005

"The Rich Promise of Two-Way Immersion"
By Kathryn J. Lindholm-Leary
Educational Leadership, December 2004/January 2005

"Louder Than Words: How K–12 World Language Teachers Are Meeting New Challenges"
By John Franklin
Curriculum Update, Fall 2004

"Versatile Technologies Broaden Students' Language Horizons"
By Rick Allen
Curriculum Update, Fall 2004

How Global Is the Curriculum?

By Andrew F. Smith

In spite of improvements in global education during the past two decades, educators and policymakers still face challenges—and now an urgent need—to educate globally literate citizens.

Global illiteracy in the United States has many causes. For most of its history, the United States has been isolated behind oceans and not threatened by its neighbors. Until the second half of the 20th century, the United States was economically self-sufficient and had little political will to get involved in the affairs of other nations.

Rapid and widespread political, economic, and military changes after World War II gave rise to issues that were global in scope, and many people became aware of the impact that events outside U.S. borders had on domestic affairs. Yet the U.S. public education system remained largely unchanged.

During the mid-1970s, educators and policymakers began to raise concerns about how well U.S. schools were preparing students for this rapidly changing world, and global education began to take shape. Most advocates did not support teaching specific global education courses because they believed that all courses should incorporate global subject matter. Nonetheless, social studies and foreign languages were the courses most amenable to integrating global perspectives.

Curriculum Shifts

In 1979, U.S. President Jimmy Carter's President's Commission on Foreign Language and International Studies[1] issued a report that set in motion four major curriculum shifts in K–12 global education.

Foreign Language Instruction

Only 8 percent of secondary school students enrolled in foreign language courses in 1979, but today approximately 50 percent do. The rapid expansion of Spanish language programs has occurred at the expense of French and German programs; other language classes, such as Chinese and Japanese—languages commonly spoken but not commonly taught—have expanded slightly. An even more significant development is the increase in foreign language programs in elementary schools—from almost none in 1979 to thousands of programs today.

Despite this solid progress, foreign language programs in the United States do not come close to comparable instruction in other countries. Japan, for example, requires four years of English language instruction (many students take more) and offers other languages as electives. Executive Director of the Joint National Committee for Languages J. David Edwards says that U.S. foreign language education during the past 20 years has moved from "scandalous to mediocre."

Geography

In 1979, geography was all but excluded from the K–12 curriculum. In 1988, the National Geographic Society established an education foundation to promote the teaching of geography. Since then, the Society has spent $110 million to support the National Geographic Bee, which this past year involved 5 million students, and to develop alliances of geography teachers and college professors concerned with improving instruction in geography from kindergarten through university; these alliances now exist in every state. In addition, four major geography organizations—the American Geographical Society, the Association of American Geographers, the National Council for Geographic Education, and the National Geographic Society—sponsored the development of national geography standards, and 48 states now have standards in geography. In 1994 and in 2002, the National Assessment of Educational Progress tested geographic knowledge and skills. The latest results showed unchanged average geography scores for 12th graders and low but improved scores for 4th and 8th graders.

World History

In 1979, few states required the study of world history in school. Those that did focused only on Western civilization. In the 1990s, the National Center for History in the Schools at the University of California at Los Angeles developed world history standards that include substantial global content. The World History Association, founded in 1982, has supported improved instruction of world history in the K–12 curriculum and helped schools develop world history courses. Two years ago, the World History Association, working with the Educational Testing Service, began summer training programs for an advanced placement course in world history, and the Educational Testing Service offered an advanced placement test in world history for the first time this year. More than 20,000 students took the exam, an all-time high for any new advanced placement subject. The National Assessment of Educational Progress will test world history within the next few years.

Public Schools with an International Focus

The fourth curriculum change has been the creation of public magnet schools with an international focus. Virtually no such schools existed in 1979, but today more than 100 have international programs, including, for example, the Bodine High School for International Affairs in Philadelphia. These schools typically require four years of instruction in foreign languages and one or two years of world history. Many specialize in extracurricular international experiences for students and teachers.

The Center for Teaching International Relations at the University of Denver has helped improve instruction and promote communications among many of these schools. Similarly, the International Baccalaureate, which was rarely offered in U.S. schools 20 years ago, is now offered in 420 schools—the largest number of participating schools in any country.

Other Opportunities
Extracurricular Activities

Independent of these formal curriculum shifts, many extracurricular activities have also strengthened U.S. students' understanding of global matters. These programs include student and teacher exchange programs, educational travel programs, Model United Nations, the Great Decisions programs sponsored by the Foreign Policy Association, and the Capitol Forum on America's Future sponsored by the Choices for the 21st Century Project at Brown University.

Technology

Many technological advances that were not even envisioned 20 years ago are now providing new opportunities for direct communication with students and teachers in other countries. Such groups as the International Education and Resource Network facilitate these contacts. Much of this communication does not take place in English, so U.S. students can practice their foreign language skills while they converse with people in other countries. In addition, many Web sites have global education materials and excellent global content for educators and students.

Challenges

As impressive as the above programs are, they reach far too few students, teachers, and schools. Even current extracurricular global programs and courses in foreign language, geography, and world history do not develop global perspectives in a comprehensive manner.

The most serious problem is inadequate teacher knowledge of the subject. Many states license teachers in social studies or history without requiring coursework in geography or world history. In elementary schools, few teachers have had any such courses. Changes in teacher licensing and preparation will help those entering the teaching profession, and those currently teaching should have access to inservice programs.

Currently, about 50 global education projects offer inservice education programs that can serve as models for new efforts. For example, the American Forum for Global Education's New York and the World project offers programs for teachers in New York City; the Center for Teaching International Relations at the University of Denver works with teachers in Colorado; and the California International Studies Project, based at Stanford University, works with colleges and universities to conduct teacher education programs throughout the state.

Another challenge is the lack of research on global education, especially on the effectiveness of particular methodologies, the proper sequencing of global concepts and skills into the curriculum, and the effects of media and newspapers on student knowledge and understanding of the world. We need a national report card on global education to evaluate our successes and failures.

We can meet these challenges. It will take the political will to expend the money and effort to set new, important priorities in the U.S. education system.

State and local boards of education should make the teaching of global content and skills an important component of education for all students.

The federal government has begun to take a leadership role by sponsoring International Education Week, which this year will take place November 18–22, and Global Science and Technology Week; these events have involved thousands of students. The federal government should also fund model global education projects and assist states and local schools in the same way that the government fostered science and mathematics education after the Soviet Union launched Sputnik in 1957.

In the wake of September 11, we need to reaffirm the importance of a globally literate citizenry. A better educated citizenry would not have responded to the September 11 attacks with such unjust retaliations as vandalizing mosques, harassing innocent Muslim Americans, or attacking Sikhs because their turbans were confused with those worn by the Taliban. We must never again find ourselves in the position, as so many did after September 11, of being unable to answer students' challenging questions.

As educators, we have a responsibility to prepare our students to meet the challenges of our increasingly, sometimes dangerously, interconnected world. It is not likely that the United States will exert global leadership for long with a citizenry that is globally deaf, dumb, and blind.

Endnote

[1]President's Commission on Foreign Language and International Studies. (1979). *Strength through wisdom: A critique of U.S. capability.* Washington, DC: U.S. Government Printing Office.

Andrew F. Smith is President of the American Forum for Global Education. 120 Wall St., Ste. 2600, New York, NY 10005; asmith1946@aol.com; www.globaled.org.

What Should Students Know About the World?

The American Forum for Global Education has published guidelines to help K–12 educators integrate global and international studies within existing academic curriculums. These guidelines focus on three possible approaches to studying the world.

Global Challenges

Global issues will not resolve themselves without deliberate action on the part of citizens who understand the complexities of these issues.

Students should leave school informed about one or more current global challenges, such as conflict and its control; economic systems; global belief systems; human rights and social justice; planet management: resources, energy, and environment; political systems; population; race and ethnicity; human commonality and diversity; the technocratic revolution; and sustainable development.

Culture and World Areas

Each person has roots in one or more cultures. Cross-cultural learning is crucial for living in a mul-

ticultural society and for understanding that other people may view the same events in profoundly different ways.

Students who study diverse cultures objectively can gain insights into their own and other cultures by examining such topics as the major geographic and cultural areas of the world; the commonalities and differences among cultures; how geography and history affect culture; and how cultures change.

Global Connections

For better or worse, this web of interconnections suffuses economic activities, religious groups, and social and community organizations.

Students should develop such skills as recognizing, analyzing, and evaluating the interconnections among local, regional, and global issues and between their personal lives and global events.

Source: Collins, H. T., Czarra, F. R., & Smith, A. F. (1996, June/July). Guidelines for global and international studies education. *Issues in Global Education,* 135/136. Available: www.globaled.org/guidelines/standards.html

Two-Way Immersion:
A Key to Global Awareness

By Elizabeth R. Howard

Two-way immersion allows students to experience the cultural and linguistic diversity of the world firsthand through integrated education settings.

Two-way immersion is an approach to education that fosters global awareness in students by deeply immersing them in a new language and culture, allowing them to experience multilingualism and multiculturalism on a personal level. These programs integrate native English-speaking students with native speakers of another language and provide academic instruction to all students through both languages. To date, there are 260 documented two-way immersion programs in the United States (Center for Applied Linguistics, 2001). Ninety-three percent of these are Spanish-English programs, and most operate at the K–5 elementary level.

All two-way immersion programs share three common goals:

■ Students will perform on grade level academically.

■ Students will develop high levels of language and literacy ability in their first and second languages.

■ Students will develop positive cross-cultural attitudes (Christian, 1994).

All education programs share the first goal. The second and third goals, however, distinguish two-way immersion from other education alternatives.

Why Two-Way Immersion?

The theoretical basis for two-way immersion is grounded in research on the education of language-minority students in the United States and on immersion education in Canada and the United States. Research indicates that language-minority students (non-native English speakers) perform better academically when provided with education in their native language (Greene, 1998; Willig, 1985), and that a strong grasp of their first language provides a solid basis for the acquisition of English literacy (Eisterhold-Carson, Carrell, Silberstein, Kroll, & Kuehn, 1990; Lanauze & Snow, 1989). Research on immersion education for language-majority students (native English speakers) shows that instruction in a second language enables students to maintain grade-level academic achievement and English literacy skills as well as acquire proficiency in that second language (Genesee, 1987; Swain & Lapkin, 1982).

Two-way immersion programs also have inherent advantages that come with integrated education settings. In most second-language programs, the teacher is the only model of that language; in two-way immersion programs, half the students serve as native language models regardless of the language of instruction. These additive bilingual instruction models allow students to develop strong skills in both the native and the second language without sacrificing mastery of the core academic content.

Central Features
Bilingualism and Biliteracy

A central feature of two-way immersion programs is the value placed on bilingualism and biliteracy. Whereas many schools in the United States have tremendous linguistic diversity because of the large influx of immigrant populations in their communities, most do not promote the long-term development of language and literacy ability in the native languages of non-native English speakers or provide extended second-language learning opportunities for their native English-speaking peers. In contrast, students in two-way immersion programs are expected to maintain and develop their first language abilities while acquiring skills in the second language. Research to date has indicated that these programs are successful in attaining this goal (Lindholm-Leary, 2001).

Cooperative Learning

Two-way immersion programs use cooperative learning as a key instructional strategy, enabling students to interact across native language groups and help one another develop strong oral and written skills in both languages while mastering academic content material. Yvonne Govea, a 1st grade Spanish teacher at Key Elementary, a Spanish-English program in Arlington, Virginia, has developed a cooperative activity for Spanish language arts instruction that yields promising results among her students. Govea forms heterogeneous groups of students comprising native speakers of each language. She gives each group a packet of word cards that correspond thematically with the class's current reading selection. The groups must then arrange the word cards, which include a selection of different parts of speech, into meaningful, grammatically correct sentences. The native Spanish speakers have the opportunity to function as group leaders in this activity because they have greater language facility and an intuitive knowledge of Spanish grammar. Students of both native language groups can work together on decoding words and discussing mechanics. Govea's use of this instructional strategy has helped develop a high level of competency in Spanish in all her students.

Cross-Cultural Understanding

Two-way immersion programs also emphasize cross-cultural understanding. Inter-American Magnet School in Chicago is a Spanish-English two-way immersion program that effectively capitalizes on the diversity of its student body to enrich the curriculum and foster cross-cultural understanding among students. For example, 5th grade students complete a unit on immigration, researching and sharing the experiences of various immigrant groups, including those represented by students in the school. This project provides the students with a deeper understanding of their peers' experiences and backgrounds.

International Exchanges

Many two-way immersion programs participate in international exchanges with sister programs in countries where the minority and majority languages are reversed. For example, Cali Calmécac Charter School, a Spanish-English program in northern California, has a sister school in Acambaro, Mexico. Every year, 8th graders from each school visit their sister school for two and one-half weeks, staying with native families and attending school with their hosts. The exchange immerses the Cali Calmécac students in Mexican culture and the Spanish language and gives them an authentic opportunity to use the linguistic and cultural skills that they have developed, as well as the chance to be cultural and linguistic brokers for their Mexican guests in the United States.

A Case Study: Alicia Chacón International School

Alicia Chacón International School in El Paso, Texas, is a highly effective example of two-way immersion. The need for multilingualism in this border region is evident because many people in the area have family in both the United States and Mexico and interact daily with people from both countries.

The student body at Alicia Chacón is largely Mexican American, but also includes sizeable numbers of European Americans and African Americans. The students are divided fairly evenly among native English speakers, native Spanish speakers, and students who are already bilingual.

Alicia Chacón's international focus is evident. The school provides instruction in a third language, in addition to English and Spanish, for 10 percent of the day to all students at every grade level. Students join language "families" by choosing to study Russian, German, Japanese, or Chinese. For the most part, native speakers teach these languages and are able to impart cultural information as well as foster language development. Students are also taken on international exchanges to further develop their linguistic and cross-cultural skills. To date, students have participated in home stays and school visits in such countries as Venezuela, China, and Germany. These exchanges give students an opportunity to advance their global awareness by living and learning in a completely different culture.

Two-way immersion education affords students the opportunity to get a glimpse of the richness and breadth of the world's diverse cultures. The best way to foster an appreciation of linguistic and cultural diversity is to give students firsthand experiences of them.

References

Center for Applied Linguistics. (2001). Directory of two-way bilingual immersion programs in the United States. [Online]. Available: www.cal.org/twi/directory

Christian, D. (1994). Two-way bilingual education: Students learning through two languages (Educational Practice Report 12). Santa Cruz, CA, and Washington, DC: National Center for Research on Cultural Diversity and Second Language Learning.

Eisterhold-Carson, J., Carrell, P., Silberstein, S., Kroll, B., & Kuehn, P. (1990). Reading-writing relationships in first and second language. *TESOL Quarterly, 24,* 245–266.

Genesee, F. (1987). *Learning through two languages: Studies of immersion and bilingual education.* Cambridge, MA: Newbury House.

Greene, J. (1998). A meta-analysis of the effectiveness of bilingual education. [Online]. Available: http ://ourworld.compuserve.com/homepages /JWCRAWFORD/greene.htm

Lanauze, M., & Snow, C. (1989). The relation between first and second language writing skills: Evidence from Puerto Rican elementary school children in bilingual programs. *Linguistics and Education, 1,* 323–339.

Lindholm-Leary, K. (2001). *Dual language education.* Clevedon, United Kingdom: Multilingual Matters.

Swain, M., & Lapkin, S. (1982). *Evaluating bilingual education: A Canadian case study.* Clevedon, United Kingdom: Multilingual Matters.

Willig, A. (1985). A meta-analysis of selected studies on the effectiveness of bilingual education. *Review of Educational Research, 57,* 363–376.

Author's Note: The work reported herein was supported under the Educational Research and Development Centers Program, PR/Award No. R306A60001 for the Center for Research on Education, Diversity & Excellence, as administered by the Office of Educational Research and Improvement, U.S. Department of Education. The contents do not necessarily represent the positions or policies of the National Institute on the Education of At-Risk Students, the Office of Educational Research and Improvement, or the U.S. Department of Education, and the reader should not assume endorsement by the federal government.

Elizabeth R. Howard is a research associate with the Center for Applied Linguistics, 4646 40th St., NW, Washington, DC 20016; www.cal.org/twi.

Language Learning: A Worldwide Perspective

By Donna Christian, Ingrid U. Pufahl, and Nancy C. Rhodes

The United States has a lot to learn from other countries about how to teach foreign languages.

In June 2004, the U.S. Department of Defense convened the National Language Conference to discuss approaches to meeting the nation's language needs in the 21st century and to identify actions that could move the United States toward becoming a language-competent nation. Participants from the government, the military, the education field, and the private sector assessed the country's needs and issued a call to action to improve its language capacity. U.S. Representative Rush Holt, a keynote speaker, maintained that the United States is in a "Sputnik moment" and needs a national commitment to languages that is

> on a scale of the National Defense Education Act commitment to science, including improved curriculum, teaching technology and methods, teacher development, and a systemic cultural commitment. (U.S. Department of Defense, 2004)

This is one of many calls for major changes in the U.S. approach to teaching foreign languages. During the two decades preceding the National Language Conference, numerous reports and articles decried the mediocrity of our students' foreign language skills and called for improved language education (National Standards in Foreign Language Education Project, 1999). In a 2003 report, the National Association of State Boards of Education (NASBE) noted the marginalization of arts and foreign language instruction and asserted that both are

at risk of being eliminated as part of the public schools' core curriculum.

The United States has not kept up with the rest of the world in providing quality foreign language instruction in its schools. How can we give our students the opportunity to develop proficiency in more than one language so that they and the broader society may benefit from expanded language competence?

Successful International Models

The practices and policies of other countries can serve as guidance. Knowledge of multiple languages is much more common and expected in countries outside the United States. One study (Pufahl, Rhodes, & Christian, 2000) collected information from educators in 19 countries: Australia, Austria, Brazil, Canada, Chile, the Czech Republic, Denmark, Finland, Germany, Israel, Italy, Kazakhstan, Luxembourg, Morocco, the Netherlands, New Zealand, Peru, Spain, and Thailand[1] More recent developments within Canada and the expanding European Union also provide models to consider.

Successful foreign language programs have several common strands.

An Early Start

Most of the 19 countries in the survey begin compulsory language instruction for the majority of students in the elementary grades, whereas schools in the United States typically do not offer foreign language classes until middle school or high school. Figure 1 summarizes the ages at which schools in the 19 countries studied introduce the first foreign language to the majority of their students.

Consider Luxembourg, for example, a multilingual country in which proficiency is expected in at least three languages. Children who do not speak Luxembourgish learn the language in compulsory preschool. All students study German beginning in

Figure 1
Foreign Languages Offered and Age of Introduction

Country	1st Foreign Language	Starting Age	Additional Languages
Australia	French	6	German, Greek, Italian, Japanese
Austria	English	6	French, Italian
Brazil	English	11 or 12	Spanish, French, German
Canada	French	10	German, Spanish, Italian, Japanese, Mandarin Chinese, Punjabi
Chile	English	>12	French, German, Italian
Czech Republic	English and German	9	French, Russian, Spanish
Denmark	English	10	German, French, Spanish
Finland	English or other	9	Swedish, Finnish, German, French, Russian, Spanish, Italian
Germany	English or other	8	French, Spanish, Russian, Italian, Turkish
Israel	English	10	Hebrew, French, Arabic
Italy	English	8	French, German, Spanish, Russian
Kazakhstan	English	10	German, French
Luxembourg	German and French	6 or 7	English, Italian, Spanish
Morocco	French and English	9 or 10	Spanish, German
Netherlands	English	10 or 11	German, French
New Zealand	French	>12	Japanese, Maori, German, Spanish
Peru	English	>12	French, German
Spain	English	8	French, German, Italian, Portuguese
Thailand	English	6	French, German, Chinese, Japanese, Arabic
United States	Spanish	14	French, German, Japanese

Source: Pufahl, Rhodes, & Christian (2000). Reprinted with permission.

1st grade. In 2nd grade, students begin spoken French; in 3rd grade, written French is added to the curriculum. In most cases, both oral and written German and French are formally taught in grades 3–6, with Luxembourgish remaining a vehicle for communication and interaction. These 7- to 12-year-olds receive one hour of instruction each week in oral Luxembourgish and an average of six to eight hours of instruction each week in German and French.

A Coherent Framework

A well-articulated curriculum and assessment framework builds coherently from one grade level to the next, from elementary school to middle school to high school to postsecondary levels. It is also standards-based and proficiency-oriented. Such a framework indicates when students should start a foreign language, how much instruction they will receive, and what levels of proficiency they should attain. The framework should also be transparent, in the sense that both educators and students should clearly understand what the levels of proficiency mean.

Most European countries have already adapted their foreign language learning and teaching at the national level to the overall frameworks and standards defined by the Council of Europe's language policy. Europe has clarified what proficiency means for at least 18 languages. This promotes consistency and coherence in language education by coordinating efforts in the various stages of education—from elementary to secondary to postsecondary—and in such sectors as public schools, private language instruction, and technical training (Nuffield Languages Inquiry, 2000). The Council's clear standards carry over into the workplace as well: Employers know what they can expect from a graduate who has achieved a certain proficiency level in a given language.

In Australia, the Australian Language Levels Project (Scarino, Vale, McKay, & Clark, 1988) influenced major national curriculum development, particularly in Chinese, Indonesian, Korean, and Japanese. It subsequently provided a framework for collaborative syllabus development and a common exit assessment from senior secondary schooling.

Strong Leadership

Leadership can come from any direction. Grassroots leadership—arising from parents and the community—often stimulates the creation of a program and can play a role in expanding and ensuring quality. Fostering strong language education programs, however, requires a solid partnership among local, state, and federal leaders because each group plays an important role in setting policy and providing funding for education.

Such leadership and collaboration might look like this: With national model standards in mind, federal funding would provide incentives for establishing and improving language programs. States would align with federal priorities by including languages in their core K–12 curriculums and providing appropriate assessments, state standards for languages, guidelines for strong professional development related to language instruction, and adequate funding. Local school districts would implement programs that follow state guidelines and support programs and teachers. Superintendents would set priorities and make funding decisions in conjunction with local school boards.

Israel has this kind of strong and coherent language education program. A new language policy, introduced in 1996 and termed "three plus" (Spolsky & Shohamy, 1999), requires the study of three compulsory languages—Hebrew, English, and Arabic—in addition to heritage, community, or other world languages.

Language as a Core Subject

Arguably one of the most influential policy decisions that countries make with respect to foreign language learning is the status of foreign languages within the school curriculum. In the 19 countries studied, 15 required at least one foreign language. Frequently, foreign languages in these countries claim the same status as mathematics, reading, and writing, and are required for school exit examinations and university entrance.

Teacher Education

As in all areas of education, well-trained teaching professionals are important contributors to excellence in language education. In some countries, such as Finland, university-based teacher education programs are highly selective, drawing teachers from a pool of the best high school graduates. Other countries, like Morocco, report that their language teachers are some of the best-trained teachers in the country. Becoming a secondary school English teacher, for example, involves obtaining a four-year degree in English from a university or teacher training college, with one year of specialization in either literature or linguistics. Students then spend a year studying language teaching methodology and getting practical training at the Faculty of Education. The majority of English teachers in universities and teacher training colleges in Morocco hold doctoral or masters degrees from British or U.S. universities. In addition to preservice preparation, inservice development for language teachers is considered one of the keys to success.

In several of the countries studied, teacher participation rates in professional development courses, seminars, and conferences are high. Many countries have an elaborate system of inservice professional development in place, with training widely available and, to some degree, required. Teachers are encouraged to attend courses and workshops, study abroad, and participate in collaborative learning—in study groups, for example—at the local school level.

In Germany, all states have systems in place that enable teachers to choose from a variety of courses offered at regional or state education centers. Each year, teachers are eligible for one week of inservice training, which the state pays for. At present, there is some discussion about making inservice training mandatory. In the Czech Republic, foreign language teachers are increasingly taking the opportunity to study abroad or attend international courses in countries with excellent reputations for foreign language teaching, such as the Scandinavian countries and the Netherlands.

Promoting Proficiency

Learning content matter through the medium of a nonnative language has become increasingly popular in many of the countries studied. Such instruction frequently occurs at the secondary school level, once students have acquired sufficient proficiency in the language. In Finland, for example, a substantial amount of content-area instruction takes place in English. A 1996 survey showed that 5 percent of elementary schools, 15 percent of middle schools, and 25 percent of high schools used this approach in some form.

In European immersion programs or bilingual programs, students—typically those in primary school—receive subject-matter instruction exclusively, or in large part, in a second language. In Canada, immersion education is a successful and widely researched practice that mainly targets the English-speaking majority learning French (Turnbull & Lapkin, 1999). The United States practices immersion education to some degree, and there has been a recent upswing in the number of two-way immersion programs, in which native speakers of two different languages (most often Spanish and English) receive instruction in both languages in the classroom.

Technology

Many of the countries surveyed are using technology to increase interaction with native speakers and improve classroom instruction. The Internet is increasingly becoming the technology of choice, with students accessing authentic materials—texts and audio/video files—in the language of study and interacting with native speakers in online chat rooms. Video-based language programs are also increasingly available. These tools can improve classroom instruction by providing access to authentic uses of the target language, increasing students' motivation to use the language, reducing students' anxiety about their performance in the language, and providing individual students with more practice in using the language than a traditional classroom setting might allow. In fact, research suggests that students produce more language—and higher-quality language—in computer-mediated contacts than in face-to-face interactions in the classroom (Leloup & Ponterio, 2003). This is another area that the United States can pursue to improve language skills outcomes.

Heritage Languages

Most countries have linguistically diverse populations with communities that speak a variety of languages. A number of respondents in the study described programs that aim to develop the mother tongue skills of members of those communities. Such programs conserve the language resources of a country and foster language achievement among minority populations.

For example, subsequent to passage of the Canadian Multiculturalism Act (1990), a number of provinces declared multiculturalism policies and established heritage language programs in their official school curriculums (Canadian Education Association, 1991; Cummins, 1991). These heritage languages include both immigrant languages—such as Cantonese, Mandarin, Portuguese, and Ukrainian—and indigenous languages, such as Inuktitut, Cree, and Mohawk. Several Canadian provinces have developed First Nations language maintenance programs to promote specific indigenous languages.

New Zealand has established *language nests* for Maori, an official language with few native speakers, and for some Pacific Island languages. Beginning at the preschool level, children are immersed in the language; later they may choose bilingual classes or special schools in which Maori is the language of instruction.

The United States has a great diversity of languages spoken within its borders. In fact, the 2000 U.S. Census documented the current use of more than 300 languages. U.S. educators can take advantage of the cultural richness of the many immigrant and indigenous communities within the United States by promoting the learning of the heritage languages spoken in these communities. One promising approach is two-way immersion, which supports continued growth in native language skills among heritage language speakers.

As Europe Sees It

In 2003, the Commission of the European Communities approved the 2004–2006 action plan, Promoting Language Learning and Linguistic Diversity. To further the goals of the European Union, the commission asserted that "the ability to understand and communicate in other languages is a basic skill for all European citizens" (Commission of the European Communities, 2003). The action plan moves that agenda forward. Among its policies and recommendations, it calls for learning "the mother tongue plus two other languages" in primary schools and carrying that study into secondary education, postsecondary education, and beyond through classroom instruction, technology-based activities, and study abroad.

The plan also focuses on improving professional development by providing teachers with greater access to travel abroad; facilitating effective teacher networks at the regional, national, and European levels; and commissioning research in language pedagogy and disseminating new findings. The plan encourages specific e-learning opportunities, such as *e-twinning,* a program in which schools from different European countries pair up to increase language learning and intercultural dialogue among students.

The plan calls for building a language-friendly environment by supporting linguistic diversity and encouraging the learning of regional, minority, and migrant languages, with specific activities, such as conferences, designed to implement these objectives. European countries have always been more attuned to the importance of language skills than the United States has been, but the coming together of the members of the European Union around such principles promises to take Europe giant leaps ahead.

A Canadian Perspective

Like the European Union, Canada has embraced language learning more enthusiastically than the United States has. In a recent policy initiative, the country rededicated itself to its goal of making its two official languages—English and French—available to all Canadians. In 2003, Canada released a five-year action plan for education, community development, and public service within a new accountability framework to promote the use of both official languages (Government of Canada, 2003). A notable objective for the education plan is to ensure that by 2013 half of all secondary school graduates are bilingual in English and French—roughly double the current number of bilingual graduates.

The Canadian government has pledged new and increased funding for programs to help schools and communities achieve these goals, committing more than $700 million to the five-year plan. This national initiative works in conjunction with an ongoing commitment to support the full array of heritage languages spoken across the country.

What's Ahead

U.S. schools and policymakers have a lot to learn from the way other countries support foreign language education. Learning languages has not been an education priority in this country in recent years. A case in point relates to assessment. A promising development in the late 1990s was including foreign language as a new subject area in the National Assessment of Educational Progress (NAEP). Yet although development of the language assessment was well on its way, the first administration of the test to 12th graders was postponed. Decisions like this underscore the fact that we have marginalized languages in the curriculum.

The American Council on the Teaching of Foreign Languages is working with colleagues around the country to celebrate 2005 as the Year of Languages in the United States (see www.yearoflanguages.org). Perhaps this initiative will raise interest in foreign language learning in communities, schools, and government agencies. We hope it will serve as the impetus for implementing some of the lessons that we have learned from other countries about foreign language education.

References

Canadian Education Association. (1991). *Heritage language programs in Canadian school boards.* Toronto, Canada: Canadian Education Association.

Commission of the European Communities. (2003). *Promoting language learning and linguistic diversity: An action plan 2004–2006.* Brussels, Belgium. Available: http://europa.eu.int/comm/education/doc/official/keydoc/actlang/act_lang_en.pdf

Cummins, J. (Ed.). (1991). Heritage languages. Special issue of *Canadian Modern Language Review, 47.*

Government of Canada. (2003). *The next act: New momentum for Canada's linguistic duality*. Ottawa, Canada: Privy Council Office, Government of Canada. Available: www.pco-bcp.gc.ca/aia/default.asp?Language=E&Page=ActionPlan

Leloup, J., & Ponterio, R. (2003). Second language acquisition and technology: A review of the research. *ERIC Digest*. Available: www.cal.org/resources/digest/0311leloup.html

National Association of State Boards of Education. (2003). *The complete curriculum: Ensuring a place for the arts and foreign languages in America's schools*. Alexandria, VA: Author.

National Standards in Foreign Language Education Project. (1999). *Standards for foreign language learning in the 21st century*. Lawrence, KS: Author.

Nuffield Languages Inquiry. (2000). *Languages: The next generation*. London: The Nuffield Foundation.

Pufahl, I., Rhodes, N., & Christian, D. (2000, December). *Foreign language teaching: What the United States can learn from other countries*. Washington, DC: Center for Applied Linguistics.

Scarino, A., Vale, D., McKay, P., & Clark, J. (1988). *The Australian language levels guidelines*. Melbourne, Australia: Canberra Curriculum Development Centre.

Spolsky, B., & Shohamy, E. (1999). *Languages of Israel: Policy, ideology and practice*. Clevedon, UK: Multilingual Matters.

Turnbull, M., & Lapkin, S. (Eds.). (1999). New research in FSL. Special issue of *Canadian Modern Language Review*, 56, 1.

U.S. Department of Defense. (2004, June 29). *National language conference results announced (News Release No. 621-04)*. Available: www.defenselink.mil/releases/2004/nr20040629-0953.html

Endnote

[1]For a comprehensive report on the study, including a summary of other comparative language education studies, see www.cal.org/resources/countries.html.

Donna Christian (donna@cal.org) is President of the Center for Applied Linguistics (CAL) in Washington, D.C. **Ingrid U. Pufahl** (ingrid@cal.org) is a Research Associate and **Nancy C. Rhodes** (nancy@cal.org) is Director of the Foreign Language Education Division at CAL.

U.S. World Language Program Models

By Audrey L. Heining-Boynton

Two program models are available to guide elementary students toward proficiency in a language other than English: the Foreign Language in the Elementary School (FLES) model or the immersion model. A district's choice depends on its linguistic goals and teacher availability.

FLES Model

The primary goal of the FLES model is language acquisition and learning about the culture of the world language studied.

■ Instruction generally begins in preschool or kindergarten and continues through elementary school.

■ The most effective programs meet for at least 30 minutes, three to five days a week.

■ Students learn grammar indirectly rather than through direct instruction.

■ Ideally, a bilingual/multilingual grade-level teacher teaches the world language. The majority of FLES programs, however, employ K–5 or K–12 licensed world language teachers.

■ Individual schools and districts usually write their own curriculums.

■ Content-enriched FLES programs use a foreign language to teach subject content from the regular school curriculum. Science and mathematics lend themselves to content-enriched FLES programs because they are laden with cognates that assist in language acquisition. A subject such as social studies, however, might require more sophisticated language.

Immersion Model

The goal of the immersion model in the United States is for students to become academically proficient in their home language as well as in the second language. Because these programs have the most contact time and teach the non-English language through regular grade-level content areas—such as science and mathematics—students can achieve the highest level of language proficiency. The three basic configurations for immersion programs are partial, total, and two-way/dual immersion.

■ In partial immersion programs, students are instructed in a language other than English for 20–50 percent of the school day.

■ In total immersion programs, teachers instruct students in all content areas in the target language, with the exception of language arts.

■ Two-way/dual immersion programs tend to be offered in a magnet school setting. Often 50 percent of students are native English speakers and 50 percent are native speakers of the additional language that will be offered at the school, such as Chinese or Spanish. Approximately half of the instructional time is in English, with the other half in the non-English language.

Audrey L. Heining-Boynton is president-elect of the American Council on the Teaching of Foreign Languages.

The Rich Promise of Two-Way Immersion

By Kathryn J. Lindholm-Leary

Two-way bilingual immersion programs go beyond language proficiency to give students academic confidence and broader cultural awareness.

Two-way bilingual immersion education has great potential to promote skills that students will need for the changing global job market and to help eradicate the achievement gap between native English-speaking and English language-learning students. Two-way programs successfully educate native English speakers and English language learners within the same classroom and fulfill for both groups the goals of full bilingualism and biliteracy, grade-level academic achievement, and multicultural competency.

There are two major reasons for helping students become bilingual:

■ *The demographic landscape of the United States is changing—and so is the job outlook.* We are rapidly becoming a country of many languages. The Latino population in the United States, for example, is expected to reach 24 percent of the general population by 2050, and the Asian American population will represent 10 percent of the population by 2050. An ever-increasing percentage of students enter school not proficient in English.

■ *Bilingual education leads to academic achievement.* Research clearly shows that students in bilingual programs can develop academic skills on a par with, or superior to, the skills of comparison groups of their peers educated in English-only classrooms (Genesee, Lindholm-Leary, Saunders, & Christian, in press; Howard, Sugarman, & Christian, 2003). Some research findings

even show that highly bilingual students reach higher levels of academic and cognitive functioning than do monolingual students or students with poor bilingual skills. In addition, students who are bilingual will have skills that enable them to take advantage of more career opportunities (August & Hakuta, 1997).

Two-Way Bilingual Immersion Defined

Two-way bilingual immersion (TWBI) programs, also known as dual language programs, instruct English language learners (ELLs) and native English-speaking students in academic content through two languages in an integrated environment (Christian, Montone, Lindholm, & Carranza, 1997; Howard, Sugarman, & Christian, 2003; Lindholm-Leary, 2001, in press). By definition, a two-way bilingual immersion program includes four crucial features:

■ Instruction and classwork take place in two languages, with the non-English language used for at least 50 percent of the students' instructional day.

■ The day includes periods of instruction during which students and teachers use only one language, with no translation or language mixing allowed.

■ Both English language learners and native English speakers do work in both languages in a balanced proportion.

■ English language learners and native English speakers are together for most content instruction.

The major goals of TWBI programs are for students to develop high levels of oral language skills and literacy in both English and the non-English language, attain academic achievement at or above grade level as measured in both languages, hold positive attitudes toward school and themselves, and exhibit knowledge about and positive attitudes toward other cultures.

Two-way bilingual immersion programs have surged in popularity in the United States. In 1987 only 37 TWBI programs operated in public schools in this country; currently, about 320 such programs exist in 25 U.S. states and in Washington, D.C., with new programs added every year. Approximately 79,000 U.S. students study in dual language programs (about half of them ELLs and half native English speakers), and in the next five years enrollment may reach 100,000. Although most of the programs are Spanish/English, other languages in the programs include Chinese, Korean, French, Portuguese, and Navajo.

Two Models of Instruction

There are two common instructional designs in TWBI programs: *90:10* and *50:50*. The allotment of time for instruction in each language varies across the grade levels in the 90:10 design but not in the 50:50. In the 90:10 model, students in kindergarten and 1st grade spend 90 percent of their instructional day with content delivered through the target, or non-English, language. Ten percent of the day is devoted to instruction in English that focuses on oral language proficiency. Reading instruction begins in the target language for native speakers of both languages.

In 2nd and 3rd grade, students spend 80 percent of their class time using the target language and 20 percent using English. As in the previous grade levels, most content is taught in the target language. In 2nd grade, English time is still largely devoted to developing students' preliteracy skills and academic language proficiency; students begin formal English reading in 3rd grade. In 4th and 5th grade, instructional time is balanced equally between English and the target language.

Unlike the 90:10 model, the 50:50 model evenly divides instructional time between the two languages across all grade levels. There are variations within this model, however. In the *50:50 simultaneous* model, reading instruction in both languages starts in kindergarten; in the *50:50 successive model*, each student initially receives reading instruction in his or her native language and begins reading instruction in the second language in 3rd grade.

For both the 90:10 model and the 50:50 model, the content areas taught in each language depend on the available curriculum and resource materials and on particular needs at each school site. However, teachers in both models attempt to give students the chance to develop academic language in all of the major curricular areas.

Factors for Success

A substantial body of literature shows similarities between the characteristics of exemplary two-way bilingual immersion programs and those of effective mainstream programs. A review of the research reveals six factors that influence the achievement of linguistically diverse students in bilingual programs (Lindholm-Leary, 2001).

School environment. A cohesive, schoolwide vision with clearly defined goals for student achievement enhances student outcomes. Administrators of bilingual immersion programs must establish faculty cohesion and collaboration within the school. In schools with a separate TWBI program, non-TWBI teachers should be informed about and urged to support the bilingual program.

Curriculum and instruction. Any effective curriculum must be clearly aligned with standards and assessment and must be both meaningful and academically challenging. The curriculum for a bilingual immersion program should integrate language instruction within the overall curriculum and foster use of both languages across the curriculum. The curriculum needs to reflect and value the cultures of all students involved, and it must provide structured and unstructured opportunities for students to speak both languages.

Program planning. A strong program-planning process should include proper scope, sequence, and alignment with developmentally appropriate practices and language proficiency levels in both languages. If the two-way bilingual program is a strand within the school, then planning for the program should be schoolwide and include non-TWBI teachers.

Assessment and accountability. TWBI education programs should use multiple measures in both languages to assess students' progress toward bilingual and biliteracy goals, along with the curricular and content-related goals.

Teacher quality and familiarity with bilingual education. High-quality teachers are vital to effective TWBI programs. Teachers must be familiar with the immersion model and with appropriate instructional strategies, and they must understand theories underlying bilingual education, second-language development, cooperative learning, assessment, and education equity. Ideally, they should be fluent in both languages.

Family involvement. Effective programs create an environment in which parents from all linguistic and cultural backgrounds feel valued and welcome. English-speaking parents should not dominate parent advisory groups to the exclusion of the non-English-proficient parents.

Rewarding Outcomes

Language Proficiency

Several studies of 5th and 6th grade students who attended a two-way bilingual immersion program since kindergarten or 1st grade show that both native English-speaking and English language-learning students became proficient in both languages (Christian et al., 1997; Howard, Christian, &

Genesee, 2003; Howard, Sugarman, & Christian, 2003). In one high school, almost all TWBI students who took the Spanish advanced placement test scored high enough to earn advanced placement credit, although native Spanish speakers had higher levels of Spanish proficiency than native English speakers did. Students in 90:10 programs tend to be more fully bilingual than students in 50:50 programs (Lindholm-Leary, 2001). Despite receiving less exposure to English during their instructional day, ELLs in 90:10 programs were as likely to be proficient in English as ELLs in the 50:50 programs were.

Reading and Writing

Two studies examining the English and Spanish reading and writing proficiency of upper-grade elementary students in Spanish/English bilingual immersion programs indicate that both groups of students progressed to high levels of reading and writing ability in both languages in composition, grammar, and mechanics (Howard, Christian, & Genesee, 2003; Serrano & Howard, 2003). Although essay-writing scores in English were similar for ELLs and native English-speaking students, ELLs tended to write more sophisticated essays in Spanish than native English speakers did. Students tended to be stronger in their first language, although the gap between ELLs' knowledge of their first and second languages was smaller. Some measures indicated that native Spanish speakers ended up with stronger writing skills in English than in Spanish.

Academic Achievement

Several investigators have examined the reading and math achievement test scores of students in two-way bilingual immersion programs at upper elementary and secondary levels to gauge the long-term impact of such programs (Collier & Thomas, 2004; Lindholm-Leary, 2001. For a review of literature, see Howard, Sugarman, & Christian, 2003). These studies show that

- Both English language learners and native English speakers in bilingual immersion programs demonstrated large gains over time in their reading and math achievement test scores.

- By middle school, both groups scored at or well above grade level in reading and math when measured in both languages.

- By 5th grade, both groups showed academic achievement at comparable or superior levels to the achievement of peers who spoke the same native language but had not gone through a bilingual immersion program.

As Figure 1 illustrates, on norm-referenced standardized tests of reading and math achievement in English, native English-speaking 7th graders in California who had completed a two-way bilingual immersion program scored above the state average for 7th graders. Students who started out as English language learners and studied through bilingual immersion not only scored significantly higher than ELLs educated in English-only classrooms but also performed on a par with native English speakers educated in English-only classrooms (Lindholm-Leary, 2004; Lindholm-Leary & Borsato, 2004, in press). Studies of youth in Chinese and Korean immersion programs yielded similar results (Lindholm-Leary, 2001).

Figure 1
Achievement of 7th Graders in Two-Way Bilingual Immersion (TWBI) Programs

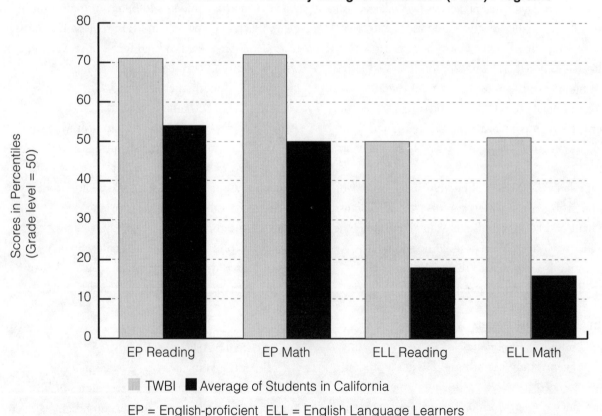

This chart compares scores on the Stanford Achievement Test of California 7th graders in bilingual immersion programs with average scores of all California 7th graders. Achievement was measured in English.

By 8th grade, ELLs educated through two-way bilingual immersion programs scored comparably to native English speakers on tests in English, regardless of whether they had participated in 90:10, 50:50 simultaneous, or 50:50 successive programs. When achievement was measured in Spanish, students in 90:10 programs received higher marks than did students in 50:50 programs (Lindholm-Leary, 2004).

Attitudes Toward School

Secondary students who studied within either a 90:10 or a 50:50 bilingual immersion program in elementary school have expressed very positive attitudes toward school and their programs (Cazabon et al., 1998; Lindholm-Leary, 2001; Lindholm-Leary & Borsato, 2001). Most students believed that learning through two languages trained them to think better and helped them do better in school. Latino students especially gave positive responses; most felt valued in the immersion program, were glad they had participated in it, and would recommend it to other students. The majority of students believed that participating in a bilingual immersion program challenged them more, gave them more confidence, and gave them a better education than a standard school model would have done—and again, Latino students expressed this view more strongly than others.

The national high school dropout rate of Latino students (30 percent) is twice the rate of that for African Americans and three times the rate of that for European Americans, and it is increasing. In one study of Latino high school students with past experience or current enrollment in TWBI programs in California, 87 percent of 9th and 10th graders and 93 percent of 11th and 12th graders interviewed said they would *not* drop out of school. Of those who had considered dropping out, most said they would remain in school because they needed an education. Almost one-half of English language-learning Latino students and one-third of native English-speaking Latino students credited the program with keeping them in school (Lindholm-Leary & Borsato, 2001).

The TWBI model represents one of the best teaching practices available to address the cultural, ethnic, and linguistic diversity in today's classrooms. These programs turn a landscape of inequality for English language learners and frustration for many teachers into a win-win situation for both schools and students. Not only is academic achievement boosted for all, but U.S. students also gain skills to survive and thrive in a country of many cultures.

References

August, D., & Hakuta, K. (1997). *Improving schooling for language-minority children: A research agenda.* Washington, DC: National Academy Press.

Cazabon, M., Nicoladis, E., & Lambert, W. E. (1998). *Becoming bilingual in the Amigos two-way immersion program.* Santa Cruz, CA: Center for Research on Education, Diversity & Excellence.

Christian, D., Montone, C., Lindholm, K. J., & Carranza, I. (1997). *Profiles in two-way bilingual education.* Washington, DC: ERIC Clearinghouse.

Collier, V. P., & Thomas, W. P. (2004). The astounding effectiveness of dual language education for all. *NABE Journal of Research and Practice, 2*(1), 1–20.

Genesee, F., Lindholm-Leary, K. J., Saunders, W., & Christian, D. (in press). *Educating English language learners: A synthesis of empirical evidence.* New York: Cambridge University Press.

Howard, E. R., Christian, D., & Genesee, F. (2003). *The development of bilingualism and biliteracy from grades 3 to 5: A summary of findings from the CAL/CREDE study of two-way immersion education (Research Report).* Santa Cruz, CA & Washington, DC: Center for Research on Education, Diversity & Excellence & Center for Applied Linguistics.

Howard, E. R., Sugarman, J., & Christian, D. (2003). *Trends in two-way immersion education: A review of the research.* Washington, DC: Center for Applied Linguistics.

Lindholm-Leary, K. J. (2001). *Dual language education.* Avon, UK: Multilingual Matters.

Lindholm-Leary, K. J. (2004). *Biliteracy issues and outcomes in different models of dual language programs.* Paper presented at the 13th Annual Illinois Reading Recovery/Descubriendo La Lectura Institute, Chicago, Illinois.

Lindholm-Leary, K. J. (in press). Review of research and best practices on effective features of dual language education programs. In L. Howard, K. J. Lindholm-Leary, J. Sugarman, D. Christian, & D. Rogers, *Guiding principles for dual language education.* Washington, DC: U.S. Department of Education & National Clearinghouse for English Language Acquisition.

Lindholm-Leary, K. J., & Borsato, G. (2001). *Impact of two-way bilingual elementary programs on students' attitudes toward school and college. Research Report 10.* Santa Cruz, CA: University of California, Center for Research on Education, Diversity & Excellence.

Lindholm-Leary, K. J., & Borsato, G. (2004). *Mathematics achievement of middle-school Hispanic students participating in two-way bilingual programs.* Paper presented at the American Educational Research Association annual meeting, San Diego, California.

Lindholm-Leary, K. J., & Borsato, G. (in press). Academic achievement. In F. Genesee, K. J. Lindholm-Leary, W. Saunders, & D. Christian (Eds.), *Educating English language learners: A synthesis of empirical evidence.* New York: Cambridge.

Serrano, R., & Howard, E. R. (2003). Maintaining Spanish proficiency in the United States. In L. Sayahi (Ed.), *Selected proceedings of the first workshop on Spanish sociolinguistics* (pp. 77–88). Somerville, MA: Cascadilla Proceedings Project.

Kathryn J. Lindholm-Leary is Professor of Child and Adolescent Development at San Jose State University, San Jose, California; 650-851-9678; klindholmleary@mac.com.

Louder Than Words: How K–12 World Language Teachers Are Meeting New Challenges

By John Franklin

Mention the words "foreign language study" to some parents, and their faces immediately tighten in apprehension. Vivid memories of spending two or three years of high school sitting through endless rote grammar assignments and vocabulary tests remain painfully fresh even after two or three decades. Once those classes ended, the knowledge—and the language—was often quickly forgotten.

Those days are gone. "People think back to when they were in high school and just memorizing words out of a textbook," says Valerie Egan, a French teacher with the Riverdale School District in Gladstone, Ore. "Now, the emphasis is on learning and *using* the language."

That emphasis on usage over grammar marks a significant turning point for language instruction. In classes where students once struggled to master verb conjugation and memorize endless lists of terms, they now strive to express themselves effectively and demonstrate their understanding of language. "When do you conjugate in a real conversation? When do you rattle off a list of vocabulary words?" asks Martha Semmer, a foreign language education project specialist in Breckenridge, Colo. "Interpersonal communication is what we emphasize now; our strategies are much more realistic."

A Practical Approach

These realistic strategies signify a change in technique and approach for teachers. "The shift has been toward communicative competence," Egan continues. "In the past, you would have a list of words giving you the names of vegetables and their translations. Now, you get questions such as, 'You're in a grocery store and need to find something, so what do you say and how do you say it?' It's all about learning to use the language effectively."

As foreign language learning becomes more prctical, however, it is also becoming less available in some areas. Pressures to improve test scores in subjects that appear on state achievement tests have led many schools to reduce or eliminate some of their language programs. "I've seen lots of language programs dwindle in the inner city," says Tod Grobey, a German teacher in Portland, Ore. When students are focused on graduating from high school rather than going to college, he says, they aren't interested in learning foreign languages.

Yet many educators are finding ways to fight this trend and keep their programs alive. Language studies, they argue, are essential to helping students understand their place in the world.

"September 11th was a wake-up call to a lot of people about the lack of foreign language [studies] in America," says Nancy Rhodes, director of foreign language education at the Center for Applied Linguistics. "People were shocked that they knew so little about the [world], and there's been much more interest in learning about other languages and cultures since then." In this context, she notes, "it's never been more important to learn a foreign language."

You *Can* Take It With You

When decision makers see the connections that language instruction makes possible, they are more likely to perceive the importance of these programs, educators say. "Few people have had pleasant experiences with foreign languages," admits Semmer. That is unfortunate, she says, because it's such a wonderful experience for students to learn what people who speak another language think. "It's those multiple perspectives that are needed to solve the many challenges our world is facing today."

Building that lifelong commitment, like any construction project, requires that a solid foundation be laid before new layers can be added. "You want students to learn to use language as a way of learning about other topics," says Anne Tollefson, a foreign language content area specialist for the Wyoming Department of Education in Casper, Wyo. "We emphasize content-based instruction now, because you don't want students learning to speak in lists of numbers and colors."

In some Wyoming classes, for example, students learn about animal habitats and behaviors in a second language as a means of tying their instruction to other subjects, such as biology or social studies. The goal is to get students to actually learn *in* the language as opposed to translating concepts from it. "I had one group of teachers showing 'Goldilocks and the Three Bears,'" Tollefson says. "The adults were learning the language with the children, and they kept wanting to know how to spell a word or count something because they needed the translation. The kids didn't; they just learned."

Although beginning foreign language instruction in elementary school may seem strange to parents who remember it as a middle or high school subject, such early instruction makes sense for numerous reasons.

"Why don't we wait until 6th grade for math instruction?" asks Rhodes. "We start it early because we know that if we start early, kids can learn it more readily. It's the same with languages." Students in kindergarten, for instance, can play with objects of different shapes and colors to teach them foreign language terms, just as they would when learning their native language. "You can roll a ball and ask, '¿Qué color es esta bola?' ('What color is this ball?') And the child can answer, 'Amarilla!' ('Yellow!')," says Rhodes. Because young children are still learning to use words, practices such as these enable them to develop proficiency at an early age. "It's

exciting for them to learn new things," Rhodes adds.

The Prime Time

But starting instruction early does more than allow students time over the course of their education to develop proficiency in a language. Recent research indicates that it also enables them to learn at a time when their brains are most readily adaptable to the task. "The research is clear that any language a child learns through age 10 is stored in one part of the brain where it can be distinguished easily," Tollefson says. "After that, it gets stored in a different part." This is why high school students and adults frequently have to switch back and forth, she continues, translating from their native language to the one that they're learning.

Learning a language at an earlier age not only makes the learning process easier for students but also helps the child connect to languages more readily. "If you start at an earlier age and get children proficient in one other language, their brains become wired for learning languages," says Mary Bastiani, a world language specialist with Portland Public Schools in Portland, Ore. "You are teaching them not just the language but language proficiency, and that makes learning a third language easier [because] you can take that ability with you."

Extending the Learning

The benefits of language proficiency extend beyond linguistics, however. According to some researchers, the skills students develop while learning a language can directly affect their performance in other subjects as well.

"Children who study foreign languages statistically outperform nonlanguage students in language, math, science, and social studies," says Carolyn Taylor, state supervisor for foreign languages at the Louisiana Department of Education in Baton Rouge. A former teacher with 15 years of classroom experience, Taylor recently participated in a statewide study of 3rd, 4th, and 5th grade students that examined how children who received 30 minutes of foreign language instruction every day fared against counterparts who received no such instruction.

"On the English language arts portion of the 4th grade Louisiana Educational Assessment Program (LEAP), 84 percent of the language kids passed the test versus 76 percent of the nonlanguage students," Taylor says. She notes another significant difference in the science rates: 80 percent of students with foreign language instruction passed, whereas 73 percent of those without the language instruction passed. The foreign language students passed the mathematics and social studies assessments at higher rates than their counterparts as well.

According to Taylor and others, using a language in a communicative setting—emphasizing how to order food in a restaurant, describe a task, discuss a video game, or simply share the details of family life with a new friend—helps students connect what they learn to their everyday lives. That, in turn, fuels an interest in learning that extends into other subjects. "If a kid studies a foreign language, those skills will carry over," says Taylor. "Administrators and policymakers need to know that the benefits of foreign language study apply outside the field."

Against the Tide

Given these benefits, one might easily expect language programs to be an essential part of a student's curriculum. The truth, however, is quite the opposite, according to educators.

"The perception in many schools is that the only core areas are language arts, math, and science, because they're the only subjects requiring assessment," says Bastiani. "No Child Left Behind says that other content areas are core subjects as well.

But many decision makers perceive everything that is not assessed as noncore, even if that's not the case."

Schools aiming to spread their resources to achieve the maximum benefit on state tests often feel pressured to allocate their limited funds toward high-priority subjects, she says. "If you look at how a school is going to be judged according to adequate yearly progress, it's going to be difficult to do something else and justify it, even if it contributes greatly not only to comprehensive education but also to . . . language arts, math, and other areas," Bastiani adds.

That core emphasis has led many schools to cut or eliminate some language programs altogether. "At the school where I taught for the last six years, I noted from my first year that there was pressure to see German get out of the way," Grobey says. "Other language teachers felt that if we could work on one language, we'd get a strong program." Those efforts culminated this past year when Grobey resigned and his school's German program was discontinued. "When I had the opportunity to go, I took it, and German was eliminated along with me," he says. "Had I stayed, there would have been pressure to not offer German the following year given the resources we had."

Grobey has since switched to another school to continue teaching German on a reduced schedule. "I'm a language guy," he says. So in his view, offering more than one language program does not mean that resources are being taken away from more prominent languages such as Spanish and French. "Students need choices," he says. "We don't serve practicality by teaching only one language."

But choice is not necessarily high on the list of some officials. "The common perception in many places is that, because of the immigration of Spanish speakers, Spanish is the most valuable language to study," says Janis Jensen, the immediate past president of the National Council of State Supervisors of Foreign Languages. "That perception has caused attrition in other languages. There's a huge enrollment in Spanish, but there's also a huge drop in other languages."

Nevertheless, sources say, different languages do thrive in some districts, often those with strong minority populations of different ethnic groups. "We don't have much concentration in Spanish," says Taylor. "Louisiana was under French rule for a number of years, so we have a very strong French culture here."

Other officials say that recent demographic changes have facilitated the introduction of many Asian dialects into school curricula. "At the K–12 level, we're seeing more Chinese and Japanese now," says Rhodes. "There's also more of an interest in Arabic as well."

Perhaps the biggest change, Rhodes notes, has come from the parents of students. Many students don't see the need for language instruction, she admits. "But more and more, parents are realizing the importance of it, and we're beginning to see a grass roots movement emerging as a result."

Taking Up the Challenge

That movement picked up steam following the 2001 terrorist attacks in the United States, educators say. "There's been a lot of effort since 9/11 to include different languages in the high school curriculum," says Janet Glass, an elementary school teacher in North Bergen, N.J. "There's also been expansion to lower levels."

In Glass's class, for example, students show their knowledge through a variety of skits designed to demonstrate their understanding of another language, as well as learning in other subjects. "I break the students into groups and have them produce a weather update entirely in Spanish," she says.

The students must introduce themselves the way an actual newscaster would on an evening news program, give the name of their "channel," and then present a weather forecast—all in Spanish.

"They even have to sign off the way a real television reporter would," Glass adds. Students also create a number of visuals to accompany the presentation, including charts, maps, and various items that can link to other units of study.

For another assignment, students order food from an actual menu featuring meals they would find in another country. Glass ties the language activity to science by requiring the students to make sure that each dish ordered links to a different level of a nutritional pyramid. "This helps keep the studies connected in students' minds," she says.

Incorporating other subjects in this manner has enabled instructors to keep programs that might otherwise have been terminated. "We as a profession have not been very prepared or thought hard about the impact of [budget cuts] on foreign language instruction," says Marcia Rosenbusch, director of Iowa State's National K–12 Foreign Language Resource Center. "A lot of people feel threatened— not radically threatened, but threatened—[because] they notice positions being eliminated or reduced, and they don't know how to respond."

Now, supporters of language learning have responded by going on the offense. In North Carolina, for example, concerned business people and parents expressed discontent about the quality of foreign language instruction students were receiving. "People were noticing that their children were graduating and going abroad without the language proficiency that they needed," says Cathie Hodges, executive director of the Alliance for Language Learning, an activist-based organization in Troy, N.C., created in response to these concerns. "Our challenge has been to convince people of the value of learning languages," Hodges adds. "Too often the programs are not seen as priorities but as frills."

As part of her role, Hodges meets each month with local officials, superintendents, and administrators to stay abreast of current legislative issues and other factors affecting foreign language programs.

She has helped teachers and parents at the district level organize and present facts to school personnel about why programs should be preserved.

"With the budget constraints we've had, a lot of districts have cut their programs," Hodges says. "But as foreign language specialists, we know that languages have to be taught at an early age and continue for a long period to develop proficiency." Making sure that educators' voices are heard, she adds, is the key to keeping foreign language programs alive.

Reaching Out

But simply keeping programs alive will not enable students to meet the needs of the 21st century, teachers say. "We know that we need lots of speakers of Mandarin, Arabic, and other languages," Tollefson says. "But we also know that there aren't enough teachers to develop those programs."

In an effort to expand capabilities and offer more language instruction to students in rural and other districts, some schools are turning to technology to overcome the lack of available instructors. In Tollefson's state of Wyoming, for example, interactive video is used to enable teachers to instruct students in more than one classroom at a time. "For our interactive Russian class, the students have been up to 500 miles apart in four or five different schools," she notes.

Although this approach is not as personal as traditional classroom instruction, it offers some benefits over chalk-and-blackboard lesson outlines. "With some cameras, students can probably see what the teacher is writing more clearly than they could with a regular blackboard," Tollefson says.

To keep the instruction personal and relevant to the students, teachers will often put school logos on display in the background and note any recent championships the schools have won. "You need to build that sense of community just the way you would in a regular classroom," she adds. "That strengthens the learning."

Bastiani, too, believes that distance learning offers a way of overcoming shortages of qualified instructors. "Wired classrooms and television instruction allow us to use a small number of people to teach 17,000 students throughout our district," she says. Like Tollefson, Bastiani says that instructors need to strive to make learning experiences as personal as possible. "We bring the kids into the videos sometimes," she notes. "We also have them compete and bring in artwork. We even celebrate their birthdays on the air."

Sharing the Challenge

Above all, educators say, the best hope for keeping language programs alive lies not in technological capabilities but with parents who get involved with their local schools and make their voices heard. In today's world, the ability to interact on a global level is increasingly important, and students can open that door by studying other languages. "We've had 200 years of monolingual thinking," says Jensen. "This needs to change."

Changing perspectives requires asking tough questions early in order to make a difference in students' lives, educators say. "What are the goals that we want for our kids?" asks Semmer. "What outcomes do we want for them at the end of their experiences? I look at the faces of kindergartners, and each of them has the potential to be bilingual or multilingual. But to do so requires a long sequence of foreign language study," she notes. "There's no such thing as learning a language quickly."

Versatile Technologies Broaden Students' Language Horizons

By Rick Allen

Portland Public Schools is carrying out an ambitious plan using technology to teach world languages. More than 17,000 elementary students in the Oregon district are studying Spanish or Japanese via distance learning TV.

"This is not just a taste of a language but a sequence that is the foundation for building proficiency in those languages," says Mary Bastiani, who heads Portland's Moshi Moshi and ¡Hola . . . Hola! Project. By the time 5th graders leave school they should be mid-level novices in either language. And, building on that, high school students who continue their language studies should graduate with at least intermediate skills that would allow them to ask for information and talk about themselves in the target language, says Bastiani.

The eight full-time teachers who broadcast live from a high school TV studio—where they also create supplemental video materials—strive for interactivity, problem solving, and cross-curricular integration using world language standards that address communication and cultural goals.

The Human Dimension

In the end, however, it's the legions of homeroom teachers helping their students prepare and reflect on the four-times-a-week live language broadcasts who have a crucial role in the success of the program, Bastiani points out. Professional development, school visits by a project liaison, and Web-based activities (available at www.moshihola.org) support the work of these classroom teachers.

"Some teachers see the value of language so much that, regardless of their ability, they're ready to become facilitators and learn the language along with the students," she notes. "We see a difference in the assessments of students whose teachers are highly motivated and those who are just 'doing it.'"

In the case of Portland, technology offers hope that all students will learn foreign languages in an era of tight school budgets and a dearth of language teachers. But technology also offers a wide range of applications and opportunities for authentic experiences of communicating in other languages or appreciating other cultures.

Cross-Cultural Exchanges

For the last four years, researchers in France have been building up an international network of student e-mail exchanges to encourage the use of technology to boost foreign language and cultural communication at the peer level, especially among early learners. Known by its acronym, MMM, which stands for Mini-Web, Multilingual, Maxi-Learning, the network can be found online at www.mmm-ec.org. The modest network involves about 1,000 students using English, French, Spanish, or Portuguese in 50 preschools or elementary schools in seven countries, including Brazil, France, Spain, and the United States.

The project's originator, Rachel Cohen, an education researcher at the University of Paris-North, believes that when even very young children use the Internet and other technologies in conjunction with learning the language and culture of another country, it bolsters their communication and written language skills in both that language and their own language. "Young kids can learn a lot, provided that the teachers do not try to teach all children the same topics at the same time but build on individual activities and personal involvement for each child," Cohen says.

Student e-mail exchanges include anything from questions about the school day, community life, holidays, and local customs, to poems and original art, says Vera Elena Fakhouri, an elementary teacher in Connecticut's Westport Public Schools. For the past two years, Fakhouri's 5th grade students at both Green's Farms Elementary and Coleytown Elementary have exchanged e-mail and "snail mail" with students at Thollon les Memises school, located in a remote village of 600 residents in the French Alps. "The exchanges have motivated students immensely and reinforced both world language and technology learning outcomes," Fakhouri notes.

At the primary school in Thollon, teacher Marik Cosson says the e-mail friendships have given her 26 10-year-olds "a true opening on the world" as they compare and contrast France and the United States and their respective cultures. When e-mails arrive in French and in English from Westport students, Cosson's students are encouraged to study English even more. Her students respond by writing letters in English that use not only phrases already familiar to them but also words "written to them by their American correspondents."

Managing the Net

Whether via e-mail or Web sites, the Internet's strength for teaching foreign languages lies in its use as a repository and channel for reading and hearing authentic language, say experts. With its millions of foreign language media sites, video clips, Web logs, and language learning sites, the Internet has become a technological resource that most foreign language teachers turn to.

Teachers can use Web sites such as Hot Potatoes (http://web.uvic.ca/hrd/halfbaked) or Quia (www.quia.com) to create interactive exercises for students at a variety of proficiency levels. To meet the needs of more advanced students, teachers can devise listening comprehension tasks using live TV or radio news broadcasts available in numerous languages at www.broadcast-live.com. Spanish language teachers can challenge their students with interdisciplinary lessons on the Internet, such as a

WebQuest that requires using Spanish and English materials to evaluate the role of Eva Peron in Argentina's history.

Although the Internet provides an abundance—some might say an overload—of authentic materials in numerous languages, experts advise language teachers to tailor Web site materials to students' ability levels to encourage instead of overwhelm. With this in mind, Spanish professor Jean LeLoup and French professor Robert Ponterio of the State University of New York at Cortland recommend using print-outs of authentic texts from the Web in the following types of activities for language beginners:

- Skimming and scanning for numbers, dates, names, and other relevant vocabulary.

- Underlining cognates, that is, words that have similar derivations in English

- Making hypotheses about text content based on an accompanying picture.

Teachers can recycle such authentic texts for more advanced activities later. That way, students' familiarity with some of the lower level vocabulary gives them confidence when they reencounter the text for more complex tasks—and teachers save time because they don't have to search the Web for new materials, suggests LeLoup. He and Ponterio are codirectors of the FLTeach: Foreign Language Teaching Forum Web site (www.cortland.edu /flteach).

Besides providing fodder for classroom lessons, the Internet also can serve as a resource when students work independently. Bilingual or multilingual dictionaries can help students find word definitions or the proper verb conjugation in an instant. But online translation software, which can translate whole passages of text in a few seconds, has caused some debate in foreign language departments.

Courtney Gosselin, who teaches Spanish at Salem High School in Salem, Mass., doesn't allow her students to use online translators, though some of her colleagues wonder whether teaching students to use them might aid their learning. Gosselin argues that, unfortunately, when students use online translators, they often avoid doing the thinking behind the translation. She has had students hand in poor machine translations that turn a word such as "can," as in "able to," into the word for a soft drink container. "The bad translations are usually how I catch them," she notes.

Video Evaluations

Gosselin prefers that students take advantage of technology in other ways, such as using digital cameras and PowerPoint software. For example, her Spanish IV students, after reading the 16th century novel *Don Quixote*, write chapters of their own in the style of the book's author, Miguel de Cervantes Saavedra. They present their new chapters in PowerPoint presentations, illustrated with digital photos of students acting out the scenes. "The point is to create an episode that shows that the student understood some concepts in the book—like attempting to right 'wrongs' even if they get themselves into a mess," says Gosselin.

With students of all ability levels, Gosselin likes to use a video camera to develop their speaking and presentation skills. First-year students do a fashion show, which reinforces Spanish vocabulary for clothing, and more-advanced students act out fables, sometimes wearing animal costumes.

Seeing themselves on video, students are more motivated to improve their language skills "because they want to sound better and look better," Gosselin says. "After they critique their footage, errors in their pronunciation register with them more than they would if I just corrected them in class."

Embracing New Technology

Every new technology that comes along seems to find a home in the foreign language classroom, experts point out. The University of Connecticut is working with a local school district to test the possibility of developing alternative assessments in the foreign language classroom by using Apple iPods, pocket-sized digital devices that can store audio and text data.

Barbara Lindsey, director of the University of Connecticut's multimedia language center, has already used iPods with her own students, and she predicts that high school students could use such technology for "man-on-the-street" interviews in authentic foreign language settings. For example, "students could do an interview at a Russian bakery in Hartford and include it in a PowerPoint presentation about Russian food," Lindsey suggests.

Professional development, more than the technology, is the critical factor in winning support for these new teaching approaches, Lindsey says. She plans to overcome such issues by giving local teachers guidance so they "can see alternative teaching strategies in action—strategies that are more focused on students communicating, collaborating, and using the language together."

APPENDIX

ACTFL PERFORMANCE GUIDELINES FOR K–12 LEARNERS

NOVICE LEARNER RANGE (GRADES K–4, 5–8, OR 9–10)

Comprehensibility: How well are they understood?

Interpersonal

- Rely primarily on memorized phrases and short sentences during highly predictable interactions on very familiar topics.

- Are understood primarily by those very accustomed to interacting with language learners.

- Imitate modeled words and phrases using intonation and pronunciation similar to that of the model.

- May show evidence of false starts, prolonged and unexpectedly placed pauses, and recourse to their native language as topics expand beyond the scope of immediate needs.

- Are able to meet limited practical writing needs, such as short messages and notes, by recombining learned vocabulary and structure to form simple sentences on very familiar topics.

Presentational

- Use short, memorized phrases and sentences in oral and written presentations.

- Are understood primarily by those who are very accustomed to interacting with language learners.

- Demonstrate some accuracy in pronunciation and intonation when presenting well-rehearsed material on familiar topics.

- May show evidence of false starts, prolonged and unexpectedly placed pauses, and recourse to their native language as topics expand beyond the scope of immediate needs.

- Show abilities in writing by reproducing familiar material.

- Rely heavily on visuals to enhance comprehensibility in both oral and written presentations.

Comprehension: How well do they understand?

Interpersonal

- Comprehend general information and vocabulary when the communication partner uses objects, visuals, and gestures in speaking or writing.

- Generally need contextual clues, redundancy, paraphrasing, or restatement in order to understand the message.

Interpretive

- Understand short, simple conversations and narratives (live and recorded material), within highly predictable and familiar contexts.

- Rely on personal background experience to assist in comprehension.

- Exhibit increased comprehension when constructing meaning through recognition of key words or phrases embedded in familiar contexts.

- Comprehend written and spoken language better when content has been previously presented in an oral and/or visual context.

- Determine meaning by recognition of cognates, prefixes, and thematic vocabulary.

Language Control: How accurate is their language?

Interpersonal

- Comprehend messages that include predominately familiar grammatical structures.

- Are most accurate when communicating about very familiar topics using memorized oral and written phrases.

- Exhibit decreased accuracy when attempting to create with the language.

- Write with accuracy when copying written language but may use invented spelling when writing words or producing characters on their own.

- May exhibit frequent errors in capitalization and punctuation when target language differs from native language in these areas.

Interpretive

- Recognize structural patterns in target language narratives and derive meaning from these structures within familiar contexts.

- Sometimes recognize previously learned structures when presented in new contexts.

Presentational

- Demonstrate some accuracy in oral and written presentations when reproducing memorized words, phrases, and sentences in the target language.

- Formulate oral and written presentations using a limited range of simple phrases and expressions based on very familiar topics.

- Show inaccuracies or interference from the native language when attempting to communicate information that goes beyond the memorized or prefabricated.

- May exhibit frequent errors in capitalization, punctuation, or production of characters when the writing system of the target language differs from the native language.

Vocabulary Use: How extensive and applicable is their vocabulary?

Interpersonal

- Comprehend and produce vocabulary that is related to everyday objects and actions on a limited number of familiar topics.

- Use words and phrases primarily as lexical items without awareness of grammatical structure.

- Recognize and use vocabulary from a variety of topics, including those related to other curricular areas.

- May often rely on words and phrases from their native language when attempting to communicate beyond the word or gesture level.

Interpretive

- Recognize a variety of vocabulary words and expressions related to familiar topics embedded within relevant curricular areas.

- Demonstrate increased comprehension of vocabulary in spoken passages when enhanced by pantomime, props, or visuals.

- Demonstrate increased comprehension of written passages when accompanied by illustrations and other contextual clues.

Presentational

- Use a limited number of words and phrases for common objects and actions in familiar categories.

- Supplement their basic vocabulary with expressions acquired from sources such as the teacher or picture dictionaries.

- Rely on native language words and phrases when expressing personal meaning in less familiar categories.

Communication Strategies: How do they maintain communication?

Interpersonal

■ Attempt to clarify meaning by repeating words and occasionally selecting substitute words to convey their message.

■ Primarily use facial expressions and gestures to indicate problems with comprehension.

Interpretive

■ Use background experience to anticipate story direction in highly predictable oral or written texts.

■ Rely heavily on visuals and familiar language to assist in comprehension.

Presentational

■ Make corrections by repeating or rewriting when appropriate forms are routinely modeled by the teacher.

■ Rely heavily on repetition, nonverbal expression (gestures, facial expressions), and visuals to communicate their message.

Cultural Awareness: How is their cultural understanding reflected in their communication?

Interpersonal

■ Imitate culturally appropriate vocabulary and idiomatic expressions.

■ Use gestures and body language that are generally those of their own culture, unless they are incorporated into memorized responses.

Interpretive

■ Understand both oral and written language that reflects a cultural background similar to their own.

■ Predict a story line or event when it reflects a cultural background similar to their own.

Presentational

■ Imitate the use of culturally appropriate vocabulary, idiomatic expressions, and nonverbal behaviors modeled by the teacher.

INTERMEDIATE LEARNER RANGE (GRADES K–8, 5–12, OR 9–12)

Comprehensibility: How well are they understood?

Interpersonal

■ Express their own thoughts using sentences and strings of sentences when interacting on familiar topics in present time.

■ Are understood by those accustomed to interacting with language learners.

■ Use pronunciation and intonation patterns that can be understood by a native speaker accustomed to interacting with language learners.

■ Make false starts and pause frequently to search for words when interacting with others.

■ Are able to meet practical writing needs, such as short letters and notes, by recombining learned vocabulary and structures. Demonstrate full control of present time and evidence of some control of other time frames.

Presentational

■ Express, describe, and narrate their own thoughts using sentences and strings of sentences in oral and written presentations on familiar topics.

■ Use pronunciation and intonation patterns that can be understood by those accustomed to interacting with language learners.

- Make false starts and pause frequently to search for words when interacting with others.

- Communicate oral and written information about familiar topics with sufficient accuracy so that listeners and readers understand most of what is presented.

Comprehension: How well do they understand?

Interpersonal

- Comprehend general concepts and messages about familiar and occasionally unfamiliar topics.

- May not comprehend details when dealing with unfamiliar topics.

- May have difficulty comprehending language supported by situational context.

Interpretive

- Understand longer, more complex conversations and narratives as well as recorded material in familiar contexts.

- Use background knowledge to comprehend simple stories, personal correspondence, and other contextualized print.

- Identify main ideas and some specific information on a limited number of topics found in the products of the target culture, such as those presented on TV, radio, and live and computer-generated presentations, although comprehension may be uneven.

- Determine meaning by using contextual clues.

- Are aided by the use of redundancy, paraphrasing, and restatement in order to understand the message.

Language Control: How accurate is their language?

Interpersonal

- Comprehend messages that include some unfamiliar grammatical structures.

- Are most accurate when creating with the language about familiar topics in present time using simple sentences or strings of sentences.

- Exhibit a decline in grammatical accuracy as creativity in language production increases.

- Begin to apply familiar structures to new situations.

- Show evidence of awareness of capitalization and punctuation when writing in the target language.

- Recognize some of their own spelling or character production errors and make appropriate adjustments.

Interpretive

- Derive meaning by comparing target language structures with those of the native language.

- Recognize parallels between new and familiar structures in the target language.

- Understand high-frequency idiomatic expressions.

Presentational

- Formulate oral and written presentations on familiar topics using a range of sentences and strings of sentences, primarily in present time but also, with preparation, in past and future time.

- May show inaccuracies as well as some interference from the native language when attempting to present less familiar material.

- Exhibit fairly good accuracy in capitalization and punctuation (or production of characters) when target language differs from native language in these areas.

Vocabulary Use: How extensive and applicable is their vocabulary?

Interpersonal

- Use vocabulary from a variety of thematic groups.

- Recognize and use vocabulary from a variety of topics, including those related to other curricular areas.

- Show some understanding and use of common idiomatic expressions.

- May use false cognates or resort to their native language when attempting to communicate beyond the scope of familiar topics.

Interpretive

- Comprehend an expanded range of vocabulary.

- Frequently derive meaning of unknown words by using contextual clues.

- Demonstrate enhanced comprehension when listening to or reading content that has a recognizable format.

Presentational

- Demonstrate control of an expanding number of familiar words and phrases and of a limited number of idiomatic expressions.

- Supplement their basic vocabulary for both oral and written presentations with expressions acquired from other sources such as dictionaries.

- In speech and writing, may sometimes use false cognates and incorrectly applied terms and show only partial control of newly acquired expressions.

Communication Strategies: How do they maintain communication?

Interpersonal

- May use paraphrasing, question asking, circumlocution, and other strategies to avoid a breakdown in communication.

- Attempt to self-correct, primarily for meaning, when communication breaks down.

Interpretive

- Identify the main idea of a written text by using reading strategies such as gleaning information from the first and last paragraphs.

- Infer meaning of many unfamiliar words that are necessary in order to understand the gist of an oral or written text.

- Use contextual clues to assist in comprehension.

Presentational

- Make occasional use of reference sources and efforts at self-correction to avoid errors likely to interfere with communication.

- Use circumlocution when faced with difficult syntactic structures, problematic spelling, or unfamiliar vocabulary.

- Make use of memory aids (such as notes and visuals) to facilitate presentations.

Cultural Awareness: How is their cultural understanding reflected in their communication?

Interpersonal

- Use some culturally appropriate vocabulary and idiomatic expressions.

- Use some gestures and body language of the target culture.

Interpretive

- Use knowledge of their own culture and that of the target culture(s) to interpret oral or written texts more accurately.

- Recognize target culture influences in the products and practices of their own culture.

- Recognize differences and similarities in the perspectives of the target culture and their own.

Presentational

- Use some culturally appropriate vocabulary, idiomatic expressions, and nonverbal behaviors.

- Demonstrate some cultural knowledge in oral and written presentations.

PREADVANCED LEARNER RANGE (GRADES K–12)

Comprehensibility: How well are they understood?

Interpersonal

- Narrate and describe using connected sentences and paragraphs in present and other time frames when interacting with topics of personal, school, and community interest.

- Are understood by those with whom they interact, although a range of linguistic inaccuracies may still exist, and, on occasion, the communication partner may need to make a special effort to understand the message.

- Use pronunciation and intonation patterns that are understandable to a native speaker unaccustomed to interacting with language learners.

- Use language confidently and with ease, with few pauses.

- Are able to meet practical writing needs such as letters and summaries by writing descriptions and narrations of paragraph length and organization, showing sustained control of basic struc-

tures and partial control of more complex structures and time frames.

Presentational

- Report, narrate, and describe using connected sentences and paragraph-length or longer discourse in oral and written presentations on topics of personal, school, and community interest.

- Use pronunciation and intonation patterns that are understood by native users of the language, although the listener/reader may on occasion need to make a special effort to understand the message.

- Use language confidently and with ease, with few pauses.

- Communicate with a fairly high degree of facility when making oral and written presentations about familiar and well-researched topics.

Comprehension: How well do they understand?

Interpersonal

- Comprehend main ideas and most details on a variety of topics beyond the immediate situation.

- Occasionally do not comprehend but usually are able to clarify details by asking questions.

- May encounter difficulty comprehending language dealing with abstract topics.

Interpretive

- Use knowledge acquired in other settings and from other curricular areas to comprehend both spoken and written messages.

- Understand main ideas and significant details on a variety of topics found in the products of the target culture, such as those presented on TV, radio, video, or live and computer-generated presentations, although comprehension may be uneven.

■ Develop an awareness of tone, style, and author perspective.

■ Demonstrate a growing independence as a reader or listener and generally comprehend what they read and hear without relying solely on formally learned vocabulary.

Language Control: How accurate is their language?

Interpersonal

■ Comprehend messages that include unfamiliar grammatical structures.

■ Are most accurate when narrating and describing in connected sentences and paragraphs in present time, with decreasing accuracy in past and future times.

■ May continue to exhibit inaccuracies as the amount and complexity of language increases.

■ Communicate successfully by applying familiar structures to new situations.

■ Rarely make errors in capitalization and in punctuation.

■ Are generally accurate in spelling or production of characters.

Interpretive

■ Deduce meaning in unfamiliar language passages by classifying words or concepts according to word order or grammatical use.

■ Apply rules of language to construct meaning from oral and written texts.

■ Understand idiomatic expressions.

■ Move beyond literal comprehension toward more critical reading and listening.

Presentational

■ Accurately formulate paragraph-length and longer oral and written presentations in present time on topics of personal, school, community, and global interest.

■ May show some inaccuracies or interferences from the native language when presentations deal with multiple time frames or other complex structures.

■ Successfully communicate personal meaning by applying familiar structures to new situations and less familiar topics, and by integrating information from audio, visual, and written sources.

■ Exhibit awareness of the need for accuracy in capitalization and punctuation (or production of characters) when target language differs from native language in these areas.

Vocabulary Use: How extensive and applicable is their vocabulary?

Interpersonal

■ Understand and often use idiomatic and culturally authentic expressions.

■ Recognize and use vocabulary from a variety of topics, including those related to other curricular areas.

■ Use more specialized and precise vocabulary terms within a limited number of topics.

Interpretive

■ Comprehend a wide range of vocabulary in both concrete and abstract contexts. Infer meaning of both oral and written texts by recognizing familiar words and phrases in new contexts.

■ Use context to deduce meaning of unfamiliar vocabulary.

- Recognize and understand the cultural context of many words and phrases.

Presentational

- Demonstrate control of an extensive vocabulary, including a number of idiomatic and culturally authentic expressions from a variety of topics.

- Supplement their basic vocabulary by using resources such as textbooks and dictionaries.

- May use more specialized and precise terms when dealing with specific topics that have been researched.

Communication Strategies: How do they maintain communication?

Interpersonal

- Are able to sustain an interaction with a native speaker by using a variety of strategies when discussion topics relate to personal experience or immediate needs.

- Show evidence of attention to mechanical errors even when these may not interfere with communication.

Interpretive

- Use background knowledge to deduce meaning and to understand complex information in oral or written texts.

- Identify the organizing principle(s) of oral or written texts.

- Infer and interpret the intent of the writer.

Presentational

- Demonstrate conscious efforts at correct formulation and self-correction by use of self-editing and reference sources.

- Sustain length and continuity of presentations by appropriate use of strategies such as simplification, reformulation, and circumlocution.

- Make use of a variety of resource materials and presentation methods to enhance presentations.

Cultural Awareness: How is their cultural awareness reflected in their communication?

Interpersonal

- Use culturally appropriate vocabulary and idioms.

- Use appropriate gestures and body language of the target culture.

Interpretive

- Apply understanding of the target culture to enhance comprehension of oral and written texts.

- Recognize the reflections of practices, products, and perspectives of the target cultures(s) in oral and written texts.

- Analyze and evaluate cultural stereotypes encountered in oral and written texts.

Presentational

- Demonstrate increased use of culturally appropriate vocabulary, idiomatic expressions, and nonverbal behaviors.

- Use language increasingly reflective of authentic cultural practices and perspectives.

Source: From ACTFL *Performance Guidelines for K–12 Learners*, 1998, Yonkers, NY: The American Council on the Teaching of Foreign Languages (ACTFL). Copyright 1998 by ACTFL. Reprinted with permission.

INDEX

ABOUT THE AUTHORS

Janis Jensen is world languages coordinator for the New Jersey Department of Education, where she is responsible for all aspects of the implementation of K–12 world languages standards, development and implementation of initiatives to facilitate systemic reform in world languages, and international education. Prior to joining the department of education, Janis taught French and Spanish at the elementary, middle, high school, and college levels.

Janis has held various leadership positions at the state, regional, and national levels. Currently, she serves as president of the National Network for Early Language Learning and immediate past president of the National Council of State Supervisors of Foreign Languages. She is also a member of the executive boards of the Foreign Language Educators of New Jersey, NJASCD, the Joint National Committee for Languages, and the National Coalition on Asia and International Studies in the Schools. She is a frequent presenter at state and national conferences and has served as a consultant on a variety of world language projects.

Most recently, she served as general advisor for the WGBH and Annenberg/CPB project, *Teaching Foreign Languages K–12: A Library of Classroom Practices*, developed in collaboration with the American Council on the Teaching of Foreign Languages (ACTFL). She currently serves on the ACTFL National Working Committee for 2005: Year of Languages.

Paul Sandrock is the consultant for world languages education at the Wisconsin Department of Public Instruction in Madison. He previously taught Spanish for 16 years in public middle and high schools.

Paul currently serves as president-elect of ACTFL and as cochair of the New Visions in Action Task Force for Curriculum, Instruction, Assessment, and Articulation.

Paul has served as president of the National Council of State Supervisors of Foreign Languages and on the boards of the Wisconsin Association of Foreign Language Teachers, the Central States Conference, the Joint National Committee for Languages, and ACTFL.

A frequent presenter at state, regional, and national conferences, Paul's has focused on implementing standards and performance assessment in world language classrooms. He was a member of the standing committee for the Foreign Language National Assessment of Educational Progress and project director for ACTFL's Integrated Performance Assessment project. Paul is the chief author of *Planning Curriculum for Learning World Languages*, a publication of the Wisconsin Department of Public Instruction.

Paul earned a master of science degree, jointly in Spanish and curriculum and instruction, from the University of Wisconsin–Madison.

ABOUT ASCD

Founded in 1943, the Association for Supervision and Curriculum Development is a nonpartisan, non-profit education association, with headquarters in Alexandria, Virginia. ASCD's mission statement: ASCD, a diverse, international community of educators, forging covenants in teaching and learning for the success of all learners.

Membership in ASCD includes a subscription to the award-winning journal *Educational Leadership*, the *Education Update* newsletter, and other products and services. ASCD sponsors affiliate organizations in many states and international locations; participates in collaborations and networks; holds conferences, institutes, and training programs; produces publications in a variety of media; sponsors recognition and awards programs; and provides research information on education issues.

ASCD provides many services to educators—prekindergarten through grade 12—as well as to others in the education community, including parents, school board members, administrators, and university professors and students. For further information, contact ASCD via telephone: 1-800-933-2723 or 1-703-578-9600; fax: 1-703-575-5400; or e-mail: member@ascd.org. Or write to ASCD, Information Services, 1703 N. Beauregard St., Alexandria, VA 22311-1714 USA. You can find ASCD on the World Wide Web at www.ascd.org.

ASCD's Executive Director is Gene R. Carter.

2005–06 BOARD OF DIRECTORS
Mary Ellen Freeley (*President*), Richard Hanzelka (*President-Elect*), Martha Bruckner (*Immediate Past President*), Donald Davis, Lavinia T. Dickerson, Margaret S. Edwards, Debra A. Hill, Linda Mariotti, Doris Matthews, Anthony Mello, Michaelene Meyer, Gail Elizabeth Pope, Keith Rohwer, Thelma L. Spencer, Sandra Stoddard, Valerie Truesdale

BELIEF STATEMENTS
Fundamental to ASCD is our concern for people, both individually and collectively.

- We believe that the individual has intrinsic worth.

- We believe that all people have the ability and the need to learn.

- We believe that all children have a right to safety, love, and learning.

- We believe that a high-quality, public system of education open to all is imperative for society to flourish.

- We believe that diversity strengthens society and should be honored and protected.

- We believe that broad, informed participation committed to a common good is critical to democracy.

- We believe that humanity prospers when people work together.

ASCD also recognizes the potential and power of a healthy organization.

- We believe that healthy organizations purposefully provide for self-renewal.

- We believe that the culture of an organization is a major factor shaping individual attitudes and behaviors.

- We believe that shared values and common goals shape and change the culture of healthy organizations.